RICHER FUTURES

RICHER FUTURES
Fashioning a New Politics

Edited by Ken Worpole

Earthscan Publications Ltd, London

First published in the UK in 1999 by
Earthscan Publications Ltd

A catalogue record for this book is available from the British Library

ISBN: 1 85383 539 0 paperback
       1 85383 538 2 hardback

Typesetting by JS Typesetting, Wellingborough, Northants
Printed and bound by Biddles Ltd, Guildford and Kings Lynn
Cover design by Yvonne Booth

For a full list of publications please contact:

Earthscan Publications Ltd
120 Pentonville Road
London, N1 9JN, UK
Tel: +44 (0)171 278 0433
Fax: +44 (0)171 278 1142
Email: earthinfo@earthscan.co.uk
http://www.earthscan.co.uk

Earthscan is an editorially independent subsidiary of Kogan Page Limited
and publishes in association with WWF-UK and the International Institute
for Environment and Development

This book is printed on elemental chlorine free paper from sustainably
managed forests

CONTENTS

Part V Dig Where You Stand

Part VI Fashioning a New Politics

ACRONYMS AND ABBREVIATIONS

BEE	*Bulletin of Environmental Education*
BSE	Bovine spongiform encephalitis
FAO	Food and Agriculture Organization (of UN)
FSC	Forest Stewardship Council
GDP	Gross domestic product
ILP	Independent Labour Party
LETS	Local Exchange Trading System
LSE	London School of Economics
NFA	National Food Alliance
NGO	Non-governmental organization
Ofsted	Office for Standards in Education
Ofwat	Office of Water Services
RCA	Royal College of Art
SAFE	Sustainable Agriculture, Food and Environment Alliance
SIDT	Solomon Islands Development Trust
SSSI	Site of Special Scientific Interest
SWIFT	Solomon Western Islands Fair Trade
TCPA	Town and Country Planning Association
UNDP	United Nations Development Programme
UNESCO	United Nations Educational, Scientific and Cultural Organization
Unicef	United Nations Children's Fund

ABOUT THE CONTRIBUTORS

Eileen Adams is Research Fellow at University College Bretton Hall and Visiting Academic at Middlesex University. Her work links art, design and environment. Her books include *Art and the Built Environment* (with Colin Ward, Longman, 1982); *Learning through Landscapes* (Learning through Landscapes Trust, 1990); *Education for Participation: Schools and the Environmental and Design Professions* (with Joan Kean, Newcastle Architecture Workshop, 1991); *Making the Playground* (Trentham Books, 1993) *Public Art: people, projects, process* (AN Publications, 1997) and *Changing Places: Young People's Participation in Environmental Planning* (The Children's Society, 1998).

Nicola Baird has an MSc in Environmental Management and works as an environmental journalist. She won the *Financial Times* David Thomas Memorial Prize in 1995. She has written four books including *The Estate We're In – who's driving car culture?* (Indigo, 1998) and the children's text *A Green World?* (Watts, 1997).

Fiona Carnie has been National Coordinator of Human Scale Education since 1991. She is a founding trustee of Bath Small School and a member of the Board of the European Forum for Freedom in Education, which is based in Germany. In 1996 she co-edited *Freeing Education: Steps towards real choice and diversity in schools* (Hawthorn Press).

Jonathan Croall was an editor in publishing with Penguin and OUP, and features editor of the *Times Educational Supplement*, before becoming a full-time writer and journalist. His books include a biography of AS Neill, an oral history of World War Two, a study of tourism and the environment, a children's novel, and *LETS Act Locally* (Gulbenkian, 1997). He is currently editor of the National Theatre's magazine *Stagewrite*, and is writing a biography of Sir John Gielgud.

David Goodway is Lecturer in History at the School of Continuing Education, University of Leeds. He specializes in nineteenth- and twentieth-century British social and cultural history and in anarchism. He has written *London Chartism, 1838–1848* (1982); and edited *For Anarchism* (1989) for the History Workshop Series, volumes of the anarchist writings of Alex Comfort and Herbert Read for Freedom Press (both 1994), and a forthcoming collection of reassessments of Herbert Read for Liverpool University Press.

Tim Lang has been Professor of Food Policy at Thames Valley University since March 1994. He is co-author of *The New Protectionism* (Earthscan, 1993), and his latest book, with Yannis Gabriel, is *The Unmanageable Consumer* (Sage, 1995) which explores the myths of consumer sovereignty.

George Monbiot was recently described by the *Evening Standard* as one of the 25 most influential people in Britain. He is the author of several investigative travel books, *Poisoned Arrows*, *Amazon Watershed* and *No Man's Land*. In 1994 he founded 'The Land is Ours' campaign. He writes a column for *The Guardian*.

Alison Ravetz trained in archaeology before becoming a historian of housing, housewives and household technology. She also writes on cities and the ideas and values expressed through built environments. Her books include *Remaking Cities: contradictions of the recent urban environment* (1980), *The Government of Space* (1986) and *The Place of Home: English domestic environments 1914–2000* (with Richard Turkington, 1995). She is now preparing a cultural history of council housing. A community activist from the anti-slum clearance campaigns of the 1970s to current schemes of urban regeneration, she has taught in several schools of architecture and is now Professor Emeritus of Leeds Metropolitan University.

Colin Ward is the author of many books on popular and unofficial uses of the environment. Several collections of his lectures to teachers, housing enthusiasts and architects are published by Freedom Press. His most recent book, *Reflected in Water: A Crisis of Social Responsibility* (Cassell, 1997), reasserts the claim for community control of water in both rich and poor countries.

Ken Worpole has been an English teacher, a community activist, a poet and writer, and the author of a number of books on urban and cultural policy, including *Saturday Night or Sunday Morning?: New Forms of Cultural Policy* (with Geoff Mulgan, 1986), *Towns for People* (1992), and a book of travel letters, *Staying Close to the River* (1995). More recently he has been responsible for a series of influential reports on aspects of the contemporary urban public realm for the think-tanks Comedia and Demos, as well as the Department of Environment.

INTRODUCTION

Ken Worpole

This book is about a new kind of politics that is emerging to fulfil the needs left unfulfilled, sometimes dangerously so, by mainstream political parties and programmes. Its starting point, however, was a common wish by a number of people active in various educational, social and environmental initiatives to pay tribute to the writer Colin Ward. This book is a tribute to him and his ideas, a kind of *festschrift* to celebrate a lifetime of industrious activity, generous friendship and support to others; his work has also exemplified a particular, and increasingly rare, quality of political hope. Ward has been one of the most quietly influential commentators on our times for more than half a century, responsible for a stream of books, pamphlets, articles, talks and lectures, on an extraordinarily wide range of topics, ranging from city childhoods, allotments, self-build housing schemes, water policy, new towns, the foyer movement, town planning, transport and anarchist theory.

In the chapters which follow, many themes first raised by Ward are further developed and elaborated by people who continue to assert the value of the informal, the voluntary, the experimental and the self-sufficient as being amongst the most considered responses to many of the pressing social issues which confront us today. Ward has been exemplary in reporting from the margins and interstices of British society where, as David Goodway makes clear in Chapter 1, many people good-humouredly beaver away at making sense of their lives and their environments, often very successfully, but with little public recognition or understanding by mainstream political theorists. He has achieved this through his long years as editor of the journal *Anarchy*, and subsequently through columns in *New Society* and *The New Statesman*, as well as his many books.

As Tim Lang notes in Chapter 8, Ward's journalistic writings have become a kind of personal conversation with others, like a bulletin board, keenly shared by a group of like-minded readers and admirers. In such ways, all societies and cultures create their own 'invisible colleges' of people, who may travel through life together without even meeting, but who do feel a genuine bond of affection and esteem from the knowledge of each other's work and writings. These elective affinities, in political life, as in personal life, are more important than we may sometimes realize, and are not without responsibilities, as any writer should know. The social responsibility involved in public writing is not widely discussed today, but I know that Colin Ward feels it keenly, only too conscious of those exhortatory political writers who urge others to the barricades or to the front line, while themselves carefully avoiding any inconvenience or danger – and in old age dismiss their youthful opinions as passing fads.

The perceived isolation of much academic thought and writing from the concerns and vicissitudes of everyday life has meant that in recent years we have witnessed a proliferation of 'think-tanks' devoted to developing ideas, particularly concerning public social policy, based on understanding 'real-life' solutions to 'real-life' problems, beyond the dependency relations of the state or the 'winners and losers' culture of the market-place. Ward himself has tended to eschew organizational processes – as one might think appropriate for an anarchist – although he has enjoyed a long association with the Town & Country Planning Association (TCPA), professionally as its Education Officer for many years, and as a regular contributor and reviewer for the TCPA journal.

Ward has disseminated ideas principally through his books, articles, talks, and personal correspondence which have all been a source of inspiration; he has given good advice on new and unusual popular initiatives and helpful bibliographical suggestions to many people, including myself and most of the contributors here. He has always been selflessly generous with his knowledge and time to many who have never met him in person. In such a long and prolific career, he has also often been ahead of his time. Invariably when people engaged in public policy work embark on a new project or field of study, they find that Colin Ward got there first, pitched camp for a while and wrote an eminently readable book on the subject.

If we can talk about a new politics of sustainability, which clearly the contributors to this book think possible, then many of its principal themes have to a large extent been prefigured in Ward's own work. Amongst the most important and enduring have been an overwhelming concern with the quality of the experience of childhood (particularly childhood play), a strong theme of the chapters in Part II by Fiona Carnie and Eileen Adams; a lifelong interest in housing issues and forms of tenant control, which the distinguished housing specialist Alison Ravetz addresses in Chapter 4, and an enthusiasm for popular self-sufficiency, which Tim Lang and Jonathan Croall describe in their analyses of current movements concerning food quality and production, and local skills exchange schemes, in Chapters 8 and 9 respectively.

Colin Ward himself contributes to this book, taking issue with the current phoney war between town and country, by seeking to describe in Chapter 5 what a working agricultural landscape would really look and feel like, while in Chapters 6 and 7 both George Monbiot and Nicola Baird – based on their own direct experiences of working in developing countries – emphasize how much we, in the so-called developed world, have to learn from countries where barter, exchange and self-sufficiency are still vital forms within the larger economy, despite the many attempts by multinational firms to impose and standardize market relations and economics upon them. In a concluding chapter I try to elaborate upon these themes and draw them together as a set of understandings and vocabularies of a new politics which is emerging on the ground, even as the mainstream political parties rush to hijack the vocabularies of self-help and mutual aid to give their programmes a more 'communitarian' gloss or spin.

I am very sorry that the historian Raphael Samuel, who was so keen to contribute to this book, did not live to do so; many of the contributors will feel the loss of his encyclopaedic knowledge of marginal social movements and histories as a personal loss, as well as a loss to the shared project which this book has become. Thanks are due to Jonathan Sinclair Wilson and Frances MacDermott of Earthscan Books, who responded to the proposal with enthusiasm and alacrity, and to Nicolas Walter for his bibliographic knowledge, advice and support. As editor, the whole undertaking has been a delight to manage and administer and never has work seemed so much like pleasure. But that was always the point of it all and of this book. There *is* an alternative to the way we conventionally do and see things.

It is hoped that these essays offer something like the beginnings of a programme for a sustainable politics in an age of social alienation and urban despair, in a world in which the most useful jobs – growing food; building houses; caring for others – are often the lowest paid or even unpaid, and in which the short-term economies of consumer mass-production put the livelihoods and environmental sustainability of future generations at grave risk. Difficult times require unusual solutions; forms of mutual aid and radical initiatives in self-sufficiency may be our only hope of handing on a world worth living in to the next generation.

PART I

People and Ideas

1 THE ANARCHISM OF COLIN WARD

David Goodway

As Ken Worpole has explained in his introduction, this book is a tribute to Colin Ward and his ideas, and Ward's influence proceeds to connect the succeeding chapters, implicitly as well as explicitly. Ward is indeed one of the great radical figures of the last thirty to forty years, but his impact has been subterranean. His name is little mentioned by commentators and is scarcely known to the wider public. A striking indication of his intellectual and institutional marginality is that he has never possessed a regular commercial publisher.

Ken Worpole has demonstrated the correspondence between Ward's concerns and contemporary debates and problems. I suspect that Ward himself would contend that this linkage can be made because of the commonsensical, realistic, necessary nature of anarchism as such (and not just his especial brand), and its relevance to the needs – political, social, economic, ecological – of the 21st century; and with this I myself would agree to a considerable extent. But equally there can be no gainsaying the very real originality of his *oeuvre*.

Colin Ward was born on 14 August 1924 in Wanstead, in suburban Essex, the son of Arnold Ward, a teacher, and Ruby Ward (née West), who had been a shorthand typist.[1] He was educated at the County High School for Boys, Ilford (whose other principal claim to fame is that for 38 years its English teacher was the father of Kathleen Raine, who was to write so venomously of him, the school and Ilford in her first volume of autobiography, *Farewell Happy Fields*). He was an unsuccessful pupil and left school at fifteen.

Arnold Ward taught in elementary schools, eventually becoming a headmaster in West Ham which, although a county borough outside the London County Council, contained the depths of poverty of Canning Town and Silvertown. He was a natural Labour supporter and the family car (a Singer Junior) was much in demand on polling days.

To grow up in a strongly Labour Party environment in the 1930s was far from stultifying as is attested by Colin Ward, having both heard Emma Goldman speak in 1938 at the massive May Day rally in Hyde Park and attended the Festival of Music for the People at the Queen's Hall in April 1939. At this festival Benjamin Britten's *Ballad of Heroes*, with a libretto by WH Auden and Randall Swingler, and conducted by Constant Lambert, saluted the fallen of the International Brigades. Ward also recalls the milk tokens, a voluntary surcharge on milk sales, by which the London Cooperative Society raised a levy for Spanish relief.

It was Ward's experiences during the Second World War that shaped, to a very large extent, his later career. His first job was as a clerk for a builder erecting (entirely fraudulently) Anderson shelters. His next was in the Ilford Borough Engineer's office, where his eyes were opened to the inequitable treatment of council-house tenants, with some having requests for repairs attended to immed-iately, while others had to wait – since they ranked low in an unspoken hierarchy of estates. He then went to work for the architect Sidney Caulfield. Caulfield was a living link with the Arts and Crafts Movement, since he had been articled to John Lough-borough Pearson (for whom he had worked on Truro Cathedral), been taught lettering by Edward Johnson and Eric Gill, and also, at the Central School of Arts and Crafts, studied under and later worked as a colleague of WR Lethaby, whom Caulfield revered.[2] Lethaby, a major architectural thinker as well as architect, is one of the nine people whom Ward was to name in 1991 as his 'influences'. Next door to his office, Caulfield let a flat at 28 Emperor's Gate to Miron Grindea, the Romanian editor of the long-running little magazine, *Adam*. It was Grindea who introduced Ward to the work of such writers as Proust, Gide, Thomas Mann, Brecht, Lorca and Canetti.[3]

On demobilization from the British Army in 1947, Ward went back to work for Caulfield for eighteen months, before moving to the Architects' Co-Partnership (which had been formed before the war as the Architects' Cooperative Partnership by a group of Communists who had been students together at the Architectural Association School). From 1952 to 1961 he was senior assistant to Shepheard & Epstein, whose practice was devoted entirely to schools and municipal housing, and then worked for two years as director of research for Chamberlin, Powell & Bon. After a career change to teaching in 1964 – being in charge of liberal studies at Wandsworth Technical College from 1966 – he returned to architecture and planning in 1971 by becoming education officer for the TCPA (founded by Ebenezer Howard as the Garden City Association) and for which he edited *BEE* the *Bulletin of Environmental Education*. He resigned in 1979, moved to the Suffolk countryside, and has ever since been a self-employed author.

Ward had been conscripted in 1942 and it was then that he came into contact with anarchists. Posted to Glasgow, he received 'a real education' on account of the eyecatching deprivation he witnessed, his use of the Mitchell Library and, as the only British city ever to have had a significant indigenous anarchist movement (in contrast to London's continental exiles and Jewish immigrants), the dazzling anarchist orators on Glasgow Green. He also frequented their Sunday-night meetings in a room above the Hangman's Rest in Wilson Street and bookshop in George Street. He was particularly influenced by Frank Leech, a shopkeeper and former miner, who urged him to submit articles to *War Commentary* in London. His first article, 'Allied Military Government', on the new order in liberated Europe, appeared in December 1943. After visiting Leech, sentenced for failing to register for firewatching and refusing to pay the fine, while on hunger strike in Barlinnie Prison, Ward, who had no clothes to wear other than his uniform, found himself transferred to Orkney and Shetland for the remainder of the war.[4]

It was in April 1945, as the war drew to a close, that the four editors of *War Commentary* were prosecuted for conspiring to cause disaffection in the armed forces. They were anticipating a revolutionary situation comparable to that in Russia and Germany at the end of the First World War, with one of their headlines insisting 'Hang on to Your Arms!' – and Ward was among four servicemen subscribers who were called to give evidence for the prosecution. All four testified that they had not been disaffected, but John Hewetson, Vernon Richards and Philip Sansom were each imprisoned for nine months (Marie Louise Berneri was acquitted on the technicality that she was married to Richards).[5] The following year, still in the army, but now in the south of England, Ward was able to report on the postwar squatters' movement in nine articles in *Freedom* (*War Commentary* having reverted to its traditional title). When he was eventually discharged from the army in the summer of 1947, he was asked to join *Freedom's* editorial group, of which George Woodcock had also been a member since 1945. This was his first close contact with the people who were to become his 'closest and dearest friends'.

This Freedom Press Group was extremely talented and energetic and, although Woodcock emigrated to Canada in 1949 and Berneri died the same year, was able to call upon contributions from anarchists like Herbert Read (until ostracized in 1953 for accepting a knighthood), Alex Comfort and Geoffrey Ostergaard and such sympathizers as Gerald Brenan. The file of *Freedom* for the late 1940s and early 1950s makes impressive reading. During the 1940s *War Commentary*, followed by *Freedom*, had been fortnightly, but from summer 1951 the paper went weekly. In 1950 Ward had provided some 25 items, rising to no fewer than 54 in 1951, but the number declined as he began to contribute long articles frequently spread over four to six issues. From May 1956 until the end of 1960, and now using the heading of 'People and Ideas', he wrote about 165 columns. Given this daunting, sparetime journalistic apprenticeship, it is hardly surprising that his stylistic vice continues to be the excessive employment of lengthy, barely digested quotations.

By the early 1950s characteristic Ward topics had emerged: housing and planning, workers' control and self-organization in industry, the problems of making rural life economically viable, and the decolonizing societies. He was alert to what was going on in the wider intellectual world, attempting to point to what was happening outside the confines of anarchism and drawing on the developing sociological literature. He wrote, sympathetically, on Bertolt Brecht (5 August and 1 September 1956) and excitedly highlighted the publication in *Encounter* of Isaiah Berlin's celebrated Third Programme talks 'A Marvellous Decade', on the Russian intelligentsia between 1838 and 1848 (25 June 1955). But who was reading his articles? *War Commentary* had fared relatively well in wartime on account of the solidarity and intercourse between the small anti-war groups, principally *Peace News*, but also the Independent Labour Party (ILP) with its *New Leader*. With the end of the war and Labour's electoral triumph in 1945, the anarchists were to become very isolated indeed – Freedom Press being unswervingly hostile to the Labour governments and their welfare legislation. Ward recalls Marie Louise Berneri saying towards the end of the forties: *'The paper gets better and better, and fewer and fewer people read it'*. The isolation and numerical insignificance of British anarchism obtained throughout the fifties also.

It was to break from the treadmill of weekly production that Ward began to urge the case for a monthly, more reflective, *Freedom* and eventually his fellow editors responded by giving him his head with the monthly *Anarchy* from March 1961, while they continued to publish *Freedom* for the other three weeks of each month.[6] Ward had actually wanted the monthly to be called *Autonomy: A Journal of Anarchist Ideas*, but this his traditionalist comrades were not prepared to allow (he had already been described as a 'revisionist'[7] and they considered that he was backing away from the talismanic word 'anarchist'), although the subtitle was initially, but largely redundantly, retained. One hundred and eighteen issues were to appear, culminating in December 1970, with a series of superb covers designed by Rufus Segar.

In a review of the 1950s and a statement of his personal agenda for the 1960s Ward had observed:

> '*The anarchist movement throughout the world can hardly be said to have increased its influence during the decade . . . Yet the relevance of anarchist ideas was never so great. Anarchism suffers, as all minority movements suffer, from the fact that its numerical weakness inhibits its intellectual strength. This may not matter when you approach it as an individual attitude to life, but in its other role, as a social theory, as one of the possible approaches to the solution of the problems of social life, it is a very serious thing. It is precisely this lack which people have in mind when they complain that there have been no advances in anarchist theory since the days of Kropotkin. Ideas and not armies change the face of the world, and in the sphere of what we ambitiously call the social sciences, too few of the people with ideas couple them with anarchist attitudes.*
>
> *For the anarchists the problem of the nineteen-sixties is simply that of how to put anarchism back into the intellectual bloodstream, into the field of ideas which are taken seriously.'*[8]

As editor of *Anarchy*, Ward had some success in putting anarchist ideas 'back into the intellectual bloodstream', largely because of propitious political and social changes. The rise of the New Left and the nuclear disarmament movement in the late 1950s, culminating in the student radicalism and general libertarianism of the sixties, meant that a new audience, receptive to anarchist attitudes, came into existence. My own case provides an illustration of the trend. In October 1961, as a foundation subscriber to the *New Left Review* (the first number of which had appeared at the beginning of the previous year) and in London again to appear at Bow Street after my arrest during the Committee of 100 sit-down of 17 September, I bought a copy of *Anarchy 8* in the Charing Cross Road at Collets. I had just turned nineteen and thereafter was hooked. When I went up to Oxford twelve months later I co-founded the Oxford Anarchist Group and one of the first speakers I invited was Colin Ward.[9] Among the members were Gene Sharp, Richard Mabey, Hugh Brody, Kate Soper and Carole Pateman. Raphael Samuel was later to tell me that he had attended some of our meetings. By 1968 Ward himself could say in a radio interview: *'I think that social attitudes have changed . . . Anarchism perhaps is becoming almost modish. I think that there is a certain anarchy in the air today . . .'*[10]

Ward's success was also due to *Anarchy's* simple excellence. This should not be exaggerated, for there was definite unevenness in quality.

> *'The editing, according to an admiring, though not uncritical contributor* [Nicolas Walter], *was minimal: nothing was re-written, nothing even subbed. "Colin almost didn't do any-thing. He didn't muck it about, didn't really bother to read the proofs. Just shoved them all in. Just let it happen".'*[11]

Ward put the contents together on his kitchen table. Coming out of *Freedom*, he frequently wrote much of the journal himself under a string of pseudonyms – John Ellerby, John Schubert (these two after the streets where he was currently living), Tristram Shandy – as well as the unsigned items. There was significant recycling of his contributions to *Freedom* in the 1950s. For example, the admired issue on adventure playgrounds (September 1961) had been preceded by a similar piece in *Freedom* (6 September 1958). Sales never exceeded 2800 per issue, there being no advance on *Freedom's* 2000 to 3000.[12]

The excellence, though, lay in a variety of factors. Ward's anarchism was no longer buried among reports of industrial disputes and comment on contemporary politics, whether national or international. It now stood by itself, supported by likeminded contributors. *Anarchy* exuded vitality, was in touch with the trends of its decade and appealed to the young. Its preoccupations centred on housing and squatting, progressive education, workers' control (a theme shared with the New Left) and crime and punishment. The leading members of 'the New Criminology' – David Downes, Jock Young (who had been a student distributor of *Anarchy* at the London School of Economics (LSE)), Laurie Taylor, Stan Cohen and Ian Taylor – all appeared in its pages. From the other side of the Atlantic the powerfully original essays by Murray Bookchin (initially as 'Lewis Herber') – 'Ecology and Revolutionary Thought' (November 1966), 'Towards a Liberatory Technology' (August 1967) and 'Desire and Need' (October 1967), all of which were later collected in *Post-Scarcity Anarchism*[13] – had their first European publication in *Anarchy*.

It was his editorship of *Anarchy* that released Ward from the obscurity of *Freedom* and Freedom Press and made his name. During the 1960s he began to be asked to write for other journals, not only in the realm of dissident politics, like *Peace News* and *Liberation* (New York), but such titles as *The Twentieth Century* and the recently established *New Society*. In 1978 Paul Barker invited him to become a regular contributor to *New Society*'s full-page 'Stand' column. When *New Society* was merged with *New Statesman* in 1988 he was retained as a columnist of the resultant *New Statesman and Society* with the shorter, but weekly, 'Fringe Benefits', until its abrupt termination by a new editor in 1996. His first books, *Violence* and *Work*, came as late as 1970 and 1972 respectively, but these were intended for teenagers and published by Penguin Education in a series edited by Richard Mabey.

Ward's third book, which appeared in 1973, was his first for an adult readership and, to date, his only work on the theory of anarchism, indeed the only one 'directly and specifically about anarchism'.[14] It is also the one that has been most translated, currently into six or seven languages, for it is, as George Woodcock considered, *'one of the most important theoretical works'* on anarchism.[15] Ward had wanted to call it *Anarchy as a Theory of Organization* – the title of an article that had appeared in *Anarchy 62* (April 1966) – but the publishers, Allen & Unwin, insisted on *Anarchy in Action*.

It is in *Anarchy in Action* that Ward makes entirely explicit the highly distinctive anarchism that had informed his editorship of and contributions to *Anarchy* during the preceding decade. His opening words – alluding to Ignazio Silone's marvellous novel, *The Seed beneath the Snow*,[16] which he remembers reading on the train back to Orkney after a leave in London – have been much quoted:

> '*The argument of this book is that an anarchist society, a society which organizes itself without authority, is always in existence, like a seed beneath the snow, buried under the weight of the state and its bureaucracy, capitalism and its waste, privilege and its injustices, nationalism and its suicidal loyalties, religious differences and their superstitious separatism.*'

His kind of anarchism,

> '*far from being a speculative vision of a future society* . . . *is a description of a mode of human organization, rooted in the experience of everyday life, which operates side by side with, and in spite of, the dominant authoritarian trends of our society*'.[17]

Acceptance of this central insight is not only extraordinarily liberating intellectually, but has strictly realistic and practical consequences:

> '. . . *once you begin to look at human society from an anarchist point of view you discover that the alternatives are already there, in the interstices of the dominant power structure. If you want to build a free society, the parts are all at hand*'.[18]

It also solves two apparently insoluble problems that have always confronted anarchists (and socialists). The first is, if anarchism (or socialism) is so highly desirable as well as feasible, how is it that it has never come into being or lasted no longer than a few months (or years)? Ward's answer is that anarchism is already partially in existence and that he can show us examples 'in action'. The second problem is, how can humans be taught to become cooperative, thereby enabling a transition from the present order to a cooperative society to be attained? Ward's response here is that humans are naturally cooperative and that current societies and institutions, however capitalist and individualist, would completely fall apart without the integrating powers, even if unvalued, of mutual aid and federation. Nor will social transformation be a matter of climactic revolution, attained in a millennial moment, but rather a prolonged situation of dual power in the age-old struggle between authoritarian and libertarian tendencies, with outright victory for either tendency most improbable.

According to this conception of anarchism, as George Woodcock observes:

> '. . . the anarchist seeks . . . not to destroy the present political order so that it may be replaced by a better system of organizing . . . Rather, anarchism proposes to clear the existing structure of coercive institutions so that the natural society which has survived in a largely subterranean way from earlier, freer, and more originative periods can be liberated to flower again in a different future. The anarchists have never been nihilists, wishing to destroy present society entirely and replace it by something new . . . The anarchists have always valued the endurance of natural social impulses and the voluntary institutions they create, and it is to liberating the great network of human cooperation that even now spreads through all levels of our lives rather than to creating or even imagining brave new world[s] that they have bent their efforts. That is why there are so few utopian writings among the anarchists; they have always believed that human social instincts, once set free, could be trusted to adapt society in desirable and practical ways without plans – which are always [constrictive] – being made beforehand.'[19]

Anarchists seek, in summary form, voluntary cooperation or mutual aid by using the means of direct action, while organizing freely. Ward is primarily concerned with the forms of direct action, in the world of the here-and-now, which are 'liberating the great network of human cooperation'. Back in 1973 he considered that

> 'the very growth of the state and its bureaucracy, the giant corporation and its privileged hierarchy . . . are . . . giving rise to parallel organizations, counter organizations, alternative organizations, which exemplify the anarchist method';

and he proceeded to itemize the revived demand for workers' control, the de-schooling movement, self-help therapeutic groups, squatter movements and tenants' cooperatives, food cooperatives, claimants' unions and community organizations of every conceivable kind.[20]

During the last 25 years he has additionally drawn attention to self-build activities (he has been particularly impressed by achievements in the shanty towns in the poor countries of Latin America, Africa and Asia), cooperatives of all types, the informal economy and Local Exchange Trading Systems (LETS). New self-organizing activities are continually emerging.

> *'Do-it-yourself is . . . the essence of anarchist action, and the more people apply it on every level, in education, in the workplace, in the family, the more ineffective restrictive structures will become and the more dependence will be replaced by individual and collective self-reliance'.*[21]

It is Ward's vision of anarchism, along with his many years of working in architecture and planning, that account for his concentration on 'anarchist applications' or 'anarchist solutions' concerning *'immediate issues in which people* are actually likely to get involved . . .'[22] Although, as he most recently tells me, *'all my books hang together as an exploration of the relations between people and their environment'* (by which he means the built, rather than the 'natural', environment), and while this clearly covers nine-tenths of his output, it seems rather (as he put it 13 years earlier) that all his publications are *'looking at life from an anarchist point of view'.*[23] So the 'anarchist applications' concern housing: *Tenants Take Over,*[24] *Housing: An Anarchist Approach,*[25] *When We Build Again, Let's Have Housing That Works*[26] and *Talking Houses;*[27] architecture and planning: *Welcome, Thinner City,*[28] *New Town, Home Town*[29] and *Talking to Architects;*[30] education: *Talking Schools;*[31] education and the environment: *The Child in the City*[32] and *The Child in the Country;*[33] education, work *and* housing: *Havens and Springboards;*[34] transport: *Undermining the Central Line*, with Ruth Rendell,[35] and *Freedom to Go;*[36] and water: *Reflected in Water.*[37]

How did Ward come to espouse such an anarchism? Who are the thinkers and which are the traditions responsible for shaping his outlook? First, it should be said that some would argue that there is no originality in Wardian anarchism since it is all anticipated by Peter Kropotkin and Gustav Landauer. There is indeed no denying Ward's very considerable debt to Kropotkin. He names Kropotkin as his economic influence; has described himself *as 'an anarchist-communist, in the Kropotkin tradition'*; and, regarding *Fields, Factories and Workshops* as *'one of those great prophetic works of the nineteenth century whose hour is yet to come'*, has brought it up to date as *Fields, Factories and Workshops Tomorrow* (1974).[38] It is also the case that Kropotkin in his great *Mutual Aid*[39] demonstrates that cooperation is pervasive within both the animal and the human worlds, in his concluding chapter giving contemporary clubs and voluntary societies, such as the Lifeboat Association, as examples. Yet Kropotkin prepared for a bloody social revolution and Ward goes far beyond him in the types of cooperative groups he identifies in modern societies and the centrality he accords to them in anarchist transformation.

Ward is still closer to the remarkable Landauer. He even goes so far as to say that his

> *'is not a new version of anarchism. Gustav Landauer saw it, not as the founding of something new, "but as the actualization and reconstitution of something that has always been present, which exists alongside the state, albeit buried and laid waste"'.*

One of Ward's favourite quotations, which he rightly regards as *'a profound and simple contribution to the analysis of the state and society in one sentence'*, derives from an article by Landauer of 1910:

> *'The state is not something which can be destroyed by a revolution, but is a condition, a certain relationship between human beings, a mode of human behaviour; we destroy it by contracting other relationships, by behaving differently'.*[40]

What this led Landauer to advocate was the formation of producers' and consumers' cooperatives, but especially of agrarian communes; and his emphasis is substantially different to Ward's exploration of 'anarchist solutions' to immediate issues. In any case, for many years Ward only knew of Landauer through a chapter in Martin Buber's *Paths in Utopia*;[41] and it is Buber (who had been Landauer's friend and editor and shared similar views concerning the relationship between society and the state but, although

sympathetic, was not an anarchist himself) whom Ward acknowledges as his influence with respect to 'society'.[42]

It seems extraordinary to me that Wardian anarchism was
nurtured within a Freedom Press Group whose other members
were looking back to the workers' and soldiers' councils of the
Russian and German Revolutions and to the collectives of the
Spanish Revolution. Ward has never believed in an imminent
revolution:

> *'That's just not my view of anarchism. I think it's unhistorical*
> *. . . I don't think you'll ever see any of my writings in* Freedom
> *which are remotely demanding revolution next week'.*

When he tried to interest his comrades in the late 1940s in a
pamphlet on the squatters' movement – to give them the idea he
had even pasted his articles up – he recalls that *'it wasn't thought*
that this is somehow relevant to anarchism'. Although they deserve
great credit for allowing him to go his own way with *Anarchy*, it
was not until after the success of *Tenants Take Over*, published by
the Architectural Press in 1974,[43] that Freedom Press suggested that
he write a book for them. The result was *Housing: An Anarchist*
Approach,[44] which, to some extent, *did* recycle his *War Commentary*
and *Freedom* pieces on postwar squatting.

Ward's difference of emphasis is, in part, to be explained by
the fact that he was approaching anarchism from a background of
architecture, town planning, the Garden City movement – 'You
could see the links between Ebenezer Howard and Kropotkin' –
and regional planning. He was considerably influenced by Patrick
Geddes (who is acknowledged in *Influences*), Lewis Mumford and
the regionalist approach. William Morris was also important, but
not for his political lectures, which are not to Ward's taste, but rather
as mediated by the Arts and Crafts Movement – his early employer,
Sidney Caulfield, had actually known Morris – and, in particular,
by Lethaby. It is Alexander Herzen, though not an anarchist, whom
he regards as his principal political influence:

> *'A goal which is infinitely remote is not a goal at all, it is a*
> *deception. A goal must be closer – at the very least the*
> *labourer's wage or pleasure in the work performed. Each*
> *epoch, each generation, each life has had, or has, its own*
> *experience, and the end of each generation must be itself . . .'*[45]

By extension, Ward was also influenced by Herzen's outstanding expositor in English, Isaiah Berlin, whose major liberal statements, *Historical Inevitability* and *Two Concepts of Liberty*, he also prizes.[46] George Orwell and his 'pretty anarchical' version of socialism need to be mentioned as well; indeed a series of five articles by Ward on 'Orwell and Anarchism', first published in 1955 in *Freedom*, have finally been reprinted.[47]

From across the Atlantic two periodicals, available from Freedom Bookshop, were important: *politics* (1944–49), edited by Dwight Macdonald in the course of his transition from Marxism to a pacifist anarchism, Ward considers *'my ideal of a political journal'*, admiring its *'breadth, sophistication, dryness'* (although Macdonald worked in London in the 1950s and 1960s Ward only met him two or three times); and *Why?* (1942–47), later *Resistance* (1947–52), edited by a group which included David Wieck and Paul Goodman. Goodman, who also contributed to *politics*, was another principal influence, firstly and always, for *Communitas*,[48] the planning classic he wrote with his brother Percival, but also for the very similar anarchism to Ward's he began to expound from 'The May Pamphlet' of 1945, included in *Art and Social Nature*.[49] Goodman became a frequent contributor to *Anarchy*, and *Anarchy in Action* is dedicated to his memory; yet Ward only met him once, when he was in London in 1967 for the Dialectics of Liberation conference. In *Anarchy 33* Ward had drawn attention to the similarities between Goodman and Alex Comfort, and the Comfort of *Authority and Delinquency in the Modern State*[50] and *Delinquency*,[51] in which he calls for anarchism to become a libertarian action sociology, is the final significant influence on Ward's anarchism.

Ward has, with good reason, been scornful of most other anarchists' obsession with the history, whether glorious or infamous, of their tradition: *'I think the besetting sin of anarchism has been its preoccupation with its own past . . .'*[52] Still, despite his own emphasis on the here-and-now and the future, he has written three historical books: *Arcadia for All: The Legacy of a Makeshift Landscape*[53] and *Goodnight Campers!: The History of the British Holiday Camp*,[54] both with Dennis Hardy; and *The Allotment: Its Landscape and Culture*[55] with David Crouch. The masterly *Arcadia for All*, a history of the 'plotlands' of south-east England, is simply a natural extension into the recent past of his major interest in self-build and squatting, and *The Allotment* touches upon similar issues. In *Goodnight Campers!* the entrepreneurial holiday camps are traced to their origins in the early twentieth century and the 'pioneer camps', in which a key role was played by the major organizations of working-class self-help and mutual aid: the cooperative movement and trade unions. The historic importance of such institutions in the provision of welfare and the maintenance of social solidarity has since *Goodnight Campers!* become a theme of increasing significance in Ward's work.[56]

Ward stated his case in 'The Path Not Taken', a striking short article of 1987.[57] Since the late nineteenth century *'the tradition of fraternal and autonomous associations springing up from below'* has been successively displaced by one of *'authoritarian institutions directed from above'*.[58] He sees a *'sinister alliance of Fabians and Marxists, both of whom believed implicitly in the state, and assumed that they would be the particular elite in control of it'* effectively combining with *'the equally sinister alliance of bureaucrats and professionals: the British civil service and the British professional classes, with their undisguised contempt for the way ordinary people organized anything'*. The result was that:

> *'The great tradition of working-class self-help and mutual aid was written off, not just as irrelevant, but as an actual impediment, by the political and professional architects of the welfare state . . . The contribution that the recipients had to make . . . was ignored as a mere embarrassment . . .'*[59]

Drawing upon several recent historical works, Ward is able to show that the nineteenth-century dame schools, set up by working-class parents for working-class children and under working-class control, were swept away by the board schools of the 1870s; and similarly the self-organization of patients in the working-class medical societies was to be lost in the creation of the National Health Service. Ward comments, from his own specialism, on the initially working-class self-help building societies stripping themselves of the final vestiges of mutuality; and this degeneration has existed alongside a tradition of municipal housing adamantly opposed to the principle of dweller control. Here we are presented with a rich, never more relevant, analysis of the disaster of modern British social policy with pointers to the way ahead if we are to stand any chance of reinstituting the self-organization and mutual aid that have been lost. Ward restates his argument in *Social Policy: An Anarchist Response*, his 1996 lectures at the LSE which summarize several of his most important themes.[60]

Colin Ward sees anarchism's best prospects in the immediate future as lying within the environmental and ecological movement. One of his greatest regrets remains that so few anarchists follow his example and apply their principles to what they themselves know best. In his case that is the terrain of housing, architecture and planning; but where, he wants to know, are the anarchist experts on, for example, medicine, the health service, agriculture and economics?

NOTES AND REFERENCES

1 All otherwise unacknowledged biographical information or quotations derive from one of three sources: a recorded conversation of 29 June 1997; an annotated bibliography of his writings prepared by Ward, July 1996 (and updated in May 1997); and correspondence with him since 1984

2 For the early career of Caulfield, who had contributed to Hampstead Garden Suburb, see A. Stuart Gray (1985) *Edwardian Architecture: A Biographical Dictionary* London: Duckworth, pp 24, 137

3 For Ward's obituary appreciation of Grindea, see *New Statesman & Society*, 8 December 1995

4 See Ward's memoir of Leech, 'Local Hero in Netherton Road', *Guardian*, 3 August 1988

5 For Ward's account, see 'Witness for the Prosecution', *Wildcat*, no 1, September 1974

6 See Ward's account in 'Foreword', Ward, C (ed) '1987', *A Decade of Anarchy, 1961–1970: Selections from the Monthly Journal 'Anarchy'*, London: Freedom Press

7 Ward, C (1990) 'Notes of an Anarchist Columnist', *The Raven*, no 12, October/December, p 316

8 Ward, C (1959) 'Last Look Round at the 50s', *Freedom*, 26 December

9 He spoke on 'Anarchism and the Welfare State' on 28 October 1963

10 Boston, R (1968) 'Conversations about Anarchism', *Anarchy*, no 85, March 1968, p 74

11 Raphael Samuel, in his exceptionally generous evaluation, occasioned by the publication of *A Decade of Anarchy*, *New Society*, 2 October 1987

12 Ward, C (1969) 'After a hundred issues', in Ward, C *Decade of Anarchy*, p 276; Boston, R (1968) op cit, Note 10, p 74

13 Bookchin, M (1974) *Post-Scarcity Anarchism*, London: Wildwood House

14 Ward, C (1986) '"I think that's a terrible thing to say!" Elderly anarchist hack tells all', in *Freedom: A Hundred Years*, Freedom Centenary Edition, October, p 63

15 Woodcock, G (1992) *Anarchism and Anarchists: Essays*, Kingston, Ontario: Quarry Press, p 231

16 Silone, I (1943) *The Seed beneath the Snow*, London: Cape

17 Ward, C (1973) *Anarchy in Action*, London: Allen & Unwin, p 11

18 Ibid, p 13

19 Woodcock, G (1992) op cit, Note 15, p 231. Woodcock was one of the most appreciative and perceptive of Ward's commentators – see also Woodcock, G (1986) *Anarchism: A History of Libertarian Ideas and Movements*, Harmondsworth: Penguin Books, 2nd edn, pp. 420–21 – but otherwise discussion of his writings has been remarkably limited, presumably because they are perceived as insufficiently theoretical. There is, however, a penetrating analysis of *Anarchy* by Stafford, D (1971) in 'Anarchists in Britain Today', in Apter, DE and Joll, J (eds), *Anarchism Today*, London and Basingstoke: Macmillan, pp 91–6. See also Miller, D (1984) *Anarchism*, London: Dent, pp 151, 205 n26, and Crowder, G (1991) *Classical Anarchism: The Political Thought of Godwin, Proudhon, Bakunin and Kropotkin*, Oxford: Clarendon Press, pp 195–6

20 Ward, C (1973) op cit, Note 17, p 137

21 Woodcock, G (1986) op cit, Note 19, p 421

22 Goodway, D (ed) (1989) *For Anarchism: History, Theory, and Practice*, London: Routledge, p 14; Ward, C (1987) op cit, see Notes 6 and 12, p 279

23 Goodway, D, p 21, n 52

24 London: Architectural Press, 1974

25 London: Freedom Press, 1976

26 London: Pluto Press, 1985

27 *Talking Houses: Ten Lectures*, London: Freedom Press, 1990

28 London: Bedford Square Press, 1989

29 *New Town, Home Town: The Lesson of Experience*, London: Gulbenkian Foundation, 1993

30 *Talking to Architects: Ten Lectures*, London: Freedom Press, 1996

31 *Talking Schools: Ten Lectures*, London: Freedom Press, 1995
32 London: Architectural Press, 1978
33 London: Robert Hale, 1988
34 *Havens and Springboards: The Foyer Movement in Context*, London: Gulbenkian Foundation, 1997
35 London: Chatto and Windus, 1989
36 *Freedom to Go: After the Motor Age*, London: Freedom Press, 1991
37 *Reflected in Water: A Crisis of Social Responsibility*, Cassell, 1997
38 Boston, R (1968) op cit, Note 10, p 65; Kropotkin, P (1985) *Fields, Factories and Workshops Tomorrow*, London: Freedom Press, 2nd edn, p iv. And Ward, with his typical modesty, writes that in a sense *Anarchy in Action* is 'simply an extended, updating footnote to Kropotkin's *Mutual Aid*' (Colin Ward, *Anarchy in Action*, London: Freedom Press, 2nd edn, 1996), p 8
39 Kropotkin, P *Mutual Aid: A Factor of Evolution*, London: Heinemann, 1902; and later editions
40 Ward, C (1973) op cit, Note 17, pp 11,19
41 Buber, M (1949) *Paths in Utopia*, London: Routledge & Kegan Paul
42 Ward, C (1991) *Influences: Voices of Creative Dissent*, Hartland: Green Books, Chap 4; Buber-Landauer-Mühsam issue *Anarchy* 54, August (1965). For Landauer see especially Lunn, E (1973) *Prophet of Community: The Romantic Socialism of Gustav Landauer*, Berkeley and Los Angeles: University of California Press; also Maurer, CB (1971) *Call to Revolution: The Mystical Anarchism of Gustav Landauer*, Detroit: Wayne State University Press; and Landauer, G (1978) *For Socialism*, St Louis: Telos Press (the only English translation of a book by Landauer – with a helpful introduction by Berman, R and Luke, T)
43 Ward, C (1974) op cit, Note 24
44 Ward, C (1976) op cit, Note 25
45 Quoted by Ward, C (1973) op cit, Note 17, p 136
46 Ward was, however, familiar with Herzen long before Berlin's broadcast 'A Marvellous Decade' in 1955. Woodcock, G (1948) had published an article on Herzen in *politics*, collected in his *The Writer and Politics*, London: Porcupine Press (Dwight Macdonald being another Herzen *aficionado*)
47 Richards, V, Ward, C and Walter, N (1998) *George Orwell at Home (and among the Anarchists): Essays and Photographs*, London: Freedom Press
48 Goodman, P and Goodman, P (1947) *Communitas: Means of*

Livelihood and Ways of Life, Chicago: University of Chicago Press
49 Goodman, P (1946) *Art and Social Nature*, New York: Vinco Publishing Company
50 Comfort, A (1950) *Authority and Delinquency in the Modern State*, London: Routledge and Kegan Paul
51 Comfort, A (1951) *Delinquency*, London: Freedom Press
52 'Colin Ward Interview', *Freedom*, June 1984
53 Ward, C and Hardy, D (1984) *Arcadia for All: The Legacy of a Makeshift Landscape*, London: Mansell
54 Ward, C and Hardy, D (1986) *Goodnight Campers! The History of the British Holiday Camp*, London: Mansell
55 Ward, C and Crouch, D (1988) *The Allotment: Its Landscape and Culture*, London: Faber and Faber
56 See, for example, 'Those Talking Co-op Blues', *Freedom*, 11 June 1994; 'A Token Anarchist's Week', *Freedom*, 29 April 1995; 'Coping with Jobless Capitalism', *Freedom*, 26 April 1997
57 Ward, C (1987) 'The Path Not Taken', *The Raven*, no 3, November, abridged as 'Rebels Finding Their Cause', *Guardian*, 12 October 1987. The apparently independently convergent views of Michael Young (in conjunction with Gerard Lemos), 'Roots of Revival', *Guardian*, 19 March 1997, were printed with an acknowledgment to Ward omitted (letter from Young to Ward, 24 March 1997)
58 Ward, C (1987) op cit, Note 57, p 195, where he says these phrases (which also appear in *Anarchy in Action*, 1973 edn, p 123) were first published in *Freedom* in 1956 (but the original printing is actually located in a long letter of 30 June 1960 to the *Listener*; and his 'Origins of the Welfare State', *Freedom*, 12 June 1959, prefigures it only weakly). His analysis of the last ten years, in fact, fleshes out and develops a longstanding preoccupation: see, for example, 'Moving with the Times . . . but not in Step', *Anarchy*, no 3 (May 1961); 'Anarchists and Fabians: An Anniversary Symposium', *Anarchy*, no 8 (October 1961); 'House and Home', *Anarchy*, no 35 (January 1964)
59 Ward, C (1987) op cit, Note 57, p 196
60 Ward, C (1996) *Social Policy: An Anarchist Response*, London: London School of Economics

PART II

Growing Up Absurd

2   EDUCATION ON A HUMAN SCALE

Fiona Carnie

INTRODUCTION

In a village on the north coast of Devon there is a small secondary school, the Small School at Hartland, which was set up by a group of parents in the early 1980s. These parents felt that it was inappropriate to send their 11-year-old children to a large secondary school 15 miles away, which would itself be bigger than the community where their children had grown up. Meanwhile, across the Atlantic, in the middle of New York City, a large failing comprehensive school has been closed and in its place a variety of much smaller schools have been opened on the same site. One of these schools, the Urban Academy, was established by a group of teachers working hard to reverse the cycle of failure experienced in particular by immigrant children from low-income families.

Both of these schools were born out of a deep concern for the growing disaffection and failure so evident within the education systems in their respective countries and a feeling that there must be a better way. And both are success stories. The truancy and drop-out rates are minimal, as are violence, bullying and vandalism, and the academic achievement of students is well above the average.

What these two very different schools have in common is a belief that education is about creating a community in which people – students, teachers and parents – have a sense of belonging and can be treated as individuals. Both are places to which young people choose to go and consequently to which they feel a commitment. They are places where young people want to learn and places in which adults feel privileged to work. And both attribute their success, at least in part, to their small size. The school in Devon has about 30 children; the school in New York has 100. These schools are very small in comparison with the other schools in their respective areas. Comprehensives in Devon have on average 1000 students. Comprehensives in New York have as many as 4000. What they show is that communities can take the education of their young into their own hands and create effective alternatives, from which mainstream provision has much to learn.

THE CRISIS IN OUR SCHOOLS

The past decade has seen education in the UK become increasingly centralized. Successive governments have sought to raise standards in schools through the implementation of a prescriptive national curriculum stipulating what children throughout the country should learn. The emphasis continues to be on academic skills and student achievement is measured in a series of tests. On the basis of these tests, league tables are drawn up which are intended to indicate the effectiveness of schools. Education has thus become a product which is delivered to children and selected by parents from a market place of schools which are set competitively against each other. Often ties to the locality are broken in the process.

Through the introduction of parental choice, families with the financial means are able to choose the school to which they send their children, as they are able to pay transport costs or even move house to be in the desired catchment area. This has had a devastating effect on many local communities and schools, particularly in inner city areas.

Underlying these reforms are the assumptions that education is predominantly about developing cognitive skills, and that learning can be measured in narrow tests. But these assumptions need to be questioned as education is about much more than academic achievement and, moreover, many of the important things which we learn are not quantifiable. By imposing a uniform and overloaded curriculum on schools the reforms have put teachers under enormous stress and made it almost impossible for them to respond to the varying needs of their students. Vast sums have been spent on these reforms, but evidence is now mounting which indicates that the aim of raising standards has not been achieved and that growing numbers of young people are being sidelined by an education system which they see as irrelevant to their lives.

In 1995–6 (the most recent year for which figures are available) over 12,000 children were permanently excluded from school (Department for Education and Employment) to add to the 100,000 disaffected young people already growing up on the fringes of society.[1] In addition there are currently about 25,000 families which have rejected school and educate their children at home, a figure that is growing fast.[2] About 10 per cent of families reject the state education system in favour of private schooling. The main reason given is the small classes and individual attention which independent schools can offer.

Most teachers and parents believe that children will do better in smaller classes. They realize that large schools, even with the best of intentions, can only be impersonal and anonymous. We know that people need to belong and to be treated as individuals. Industry is responding to this human need by organizing employees in teams or groups: the education world, too, needs to take the question of size seriously.

Of course smaller structures on their own do not provide the answer to the many problems in the education system. But evidence and experience increasingly demonstrate that smaller size is a precondition for effective learning. This chapter will explore what education is for, how smaller structures enable schools to be more effective and how the education system can and should be opened up to encourage new experiments.

WHAT IS EDUCATION FOR?

One problem with education is that there is little consensus about its purpose. The first public (state) schools were established to educate the masses for work in factories. They aimed to produce people who could follow instructions and carry out straightforward tasks reliably. A system of schooling was thus developed which was primarily geared to the requirements of the economy, subjugating the needs of the individual child. Society has changed dramatically since that time, and the kind of jobs for which people were being educated are fast disappearing. However, this has not had a significant impact on the way in which schooling is currently organized. Consequently we are left with an outdated system based on too narrow a view of education and which does not adequately equip young people for life in contemporary society.

It is time to develop a much broader vision for education, one which takes account of the kind of people who will enable society to flourish in the twenty-first century. An education which encourages young people to be thoughtful and questioning, to be resourceful and able to take initiative, to be caring and with a strong moral sense is more likely to produce the kind of people able to regenerate society from the grass roots than one which focuses narrowly on academic achievement. Crispin Tickell,[3] a former UK representative to the United Nations, states that the aim of education must be:

> '*to produce citizens able to develop their potentialities both as individuals and members of the community, to live in reasonable harmony with their surroundings, to think for themselves and to cope with problems as we can now foresee them*'.

It follows from this that the role of the school is to motivate young people to learn, to empower them to participate in decision making and enable them to create a sustainable world as well as to prepare them for the world of work. These different elements are all inter-connected and must be woven together in the design of a coherent system.

EDUCATION FOR A SUSTAINABLE WORLD

The crisis in the education system is evidence of its failure to respond to the changing world in a way which addresses the challenges of our time. As the American environmental educator, David Orr[4] has observed, education *per se* is not necessarily a good thing. The designer of the atom bomb and the perpetrators of Auschwitz and Dachau were not ignorant people. His point is that:

> '*education is no guarantee of decency, prudence or wisdom. More of the same kind of education will only compound our problems. This is not an argument for ignorance but rather a statement that the worth of education must now be measured against the standards of decency and human survival – the issues now looming so large before us in the twenty-first*

century. It is not education, but education of a certain kind,
that will save us.'

It is the values of western, consumerist society which dominate
the school system and in the words of the environmentalist, Stephen
Sterling,[5] *'logically, education that reproduces modernism uncritically*
cannot effectively be engaged in resolving the crises modernism has
created'. We need a new set of values to underpin education: a set
of values which places the child at the centre of the education
process and which will bring together ethos, organization, curriculum and methods as a coherent whole. In other words, an
education in which what children learn, how they learn and the
organizational context in which learning takes place all support
each other. An approach to education which achieves this is far
more likely to give meaning and enable children to make sense of
their world and their experiences.

In order to address the growing ecological crisis to which David
Orr refers, environmental concerns must inform the policy and
practice of schools. And yet, as Eileen Adams points out in Chapter
3, environmental education is seen as an optional extra. Young
people are taught about the environment in schools which, as
organizations, do very little to conserve natural resources. Mostly
they do not recycle; they are not energy efficient; they do not buy
food from local producers. Students are taught about healthy diet
and are then served mass-produced food for their lunch. Machines
selling Coca-Cola and crisps are a regular feature of school
corridors. Children are taught about improving their local environment in classrooms with leaking roofs, cracked windows and
peeling paintwork. The chasm between theory and practice makes
a mockery of any attempt to instil in young people a sense that,
through their own efforts, they can make a difference to their world.
What they are being taught and what they are experiencing do
not add up.

We know that we learn most through personal experience. It is
vital therefore that the education process connects young people
with their environment rather than cutting them off from it. In a
world in which children are watching two to three hours of
television each day, playing endless computer games and being
ferried everywhere by car, they need to go outside and get dirty.
According to John Taylor Gatto,[6] New York Teacher-of-the-Year for
two consecutive years, *'if there is to be any hope for the planet children*

need to get out there and experience it'. It is time for the walls between school and the world beyond to be knocked down, so that the world becomes the classroom and learning is seen as part of life, not separated from it.

Royton and Crompton Comprehensive School in Oldham is working to integrate the environmental theme and has introduced a whole-school cross-curricular commitment to Education for Sustainability. In history for example, children are given the chance to debate and compare periods of history taking into account the concept of 'quality of life', an important issue for environmentalists which is also discussed in Chapter 10. Using the Index of Sustainable Economic Welfare, a quality-of-life indicator which includes not only economic factors but also social and environmental ones, pupils are invited to challenge the idea of history as the straightforward onward and upward march of progress. Concepts such as power, law, morality, happiness, individualism and community are among topics raised and debated by the children.

But changes to the curriculum must be reflected in school policy. The Small School at Hartland is committed to promoting environmental sustainability in a consistent manner, and teaching practices, materials and premises reflect this commitment. Staff and students have carried out an energy audit of the buildings and an environmental audit of the grounds. Recommendations from the audits are being put into place. There is no good reason why other schools and universities should not follow suit.

It is the experience of our environment that gives us a sense of who and what we are and so this has to be the starting point for the education process. For education to help young people envision and shape the future, school must build on this experience and encourage children to think critically about the world, to make decisions based on their thinking and to take responsibility for those decisions. Only then is there any chance of creating a fairer and more sustainable world. How can the education process begin to achieve these things?

EDUCATION FOR LEARNING

First and foremost education must be about engaging the child so that he or she becomes personally involved in learning. This means personalizing the education process so that it is appropriate for each child, taking account of his or her interests, abilities and also local surroundings.

Too many children are turned off learning, either because they are not inspired by the content or it is not at the right level for them. How often do we hear young people dismiss school as boring? This perception is at the heart of educational failure and unless it is addressed, and schools are turned into places to which young people want to go, the system will fail our young in increasing numbers. If we are to create a 'learning society' it is essential to make learning into a positive experience for all children.

For children to learn, they have to be motivated and this requires that they are known individually by teachers who understand not only their interests but also how they learn. Harvard professor Howard Gardner[7] has suggested that there are different kinds of intelligence which indicate that people learn in different ways. These intelligences include logical/mathematical, linguistic, musical, spatial, bodily/kinaesthetic, interpersonal and intrapersonal, and it has since been suggested that an eighth – natural or ecological intelligence – be added. Because traditional methods of learning rely predominantly on skills of logic and rationality they hinder the vast majority of people who are intelligent in different ways. For children to be able to learn and to succeed in learning, the process must be tailored to build on their individual strengths rather than expose them continually to their weaknesses.

It is impossible, however, with classes of 30 children or more, for teachers to know their students individually and respond to their differing learning needs. Furthermore, schools have been encouraged to use whole-class and didactic methods of instruction which inevitably ignore these differences.

Advances in what we know about how the brain works and in new learning technologies point towards a more independent style of learning. Whilst there is a need to exercise caution in the extent to which computers are used to support learning there is little doubt that used wisely they have the potential to revolutionize the way in which education is organized. With an emphasis on self-direction, learning can take place in a range of different places and at the appropriate speed and level for each learner. The role of the teacher can thus change from deliverer of information to that of mentor and coach.

The East Midlands Flexi College in Burton-upon-Trent exemplifies a more flexible and individual approach. Students each have their own learning plans and their timetable includes time for home or library study. Such an approach allows much greater flexibility in the way in which education is offered to children. The Flexi College is open long hours to fit in with parents' different work patterns.

The move away from coercion and control towards motivation and a sense of autonomy is crucial in the drive to encourage learning. A likely effect of such an approach is that fewer areas are covered, but that they are covered in greater depth. However, a curriculum based on quality and in-depth understanding is preferable to one based on a superficial skim through a wide range of subject areas. The word education comes from the Latin *educare*, meaning to draw out – drawing out a child's interest and enthusiasm, not shovelling in a load of facts. This is the information age after all: we can get all the facts we need. What children really need to know is how to make sense of it all and that comes through careful guidance and support from teachers who know their students well.

The point is that learning cannot be compartmentalized. Instead it must help young people make sense of their world by showing the connections, not the differences, between subject areas and by relating these to their own lives. A curriculum based on topics or themes relating to each other and to real world issues is far more likely to reach children than one based on abstract academic disciplines.

The starting point has to be the child and the process must involve prompting children to think critically about issues which affect them rather than blandly receiving a package of knowledge delivered by teachers. It was Tolstoy who said that the only real object of education is to leave a man (sic) in the condition of continually asking questions. For education to encourage personal development, it has to positively and actively engage children in this way.

EDUCATION FOR DEMOCRACY

Secondly, education should be about empowering young people to contribute to and participate in society, thereby learning that they can shape their world and that they have a role in creating a more sustainable future. To begin to achieve this, young people must be given a say and be involved in decisions about things which affect them.

School, as it is currently organized, is a disempowering experience. Students are told what to learn, they are told what to wear and they are told how to behave. Teachers are even told what to teach. Schools should be helping young people towards independence, encouraging them to work collaboratively to take decisions and responsibility for those decisions. They will make mistakes, of course, but they will learn from those mistakes.

A growing number of schools, with a nod to promoting democratic behaviour, have introduced school councils, but these are generally only allowed to discuss trivial matters. Instead, children should be involved in real decisions about, for example, what should be sold in the school cafeteria, or how the school grounds should be used. The discussion and decisions about these issues should be closely related to what they are learning. By involving young people directly in making decisions and taking responsibility for a much broader and deeper range of issues they would be given a sense of ownership of their learning and of their school environment.

Highfield Junior School in Plymouth gives its children a more extensive role than most in running the school. The children have an input into decisions about choosing new staff, dealing with disruptive children and buying new furniture. It was previously a sink school, but has been turned round as the children have acquired a real commitment to making it work. They now feel that it is their school. But Highfield Junior doesn't go far enough. The content of learning should also be decided by all who are directly involved in a school – pupils, teachers and parents. The issues facing children growing up in tower blocks on an inner city estate are very different from those facing children in a remote rural situation and schools need the freedom to be able to respond to these differences.

There are other models: in a number of schools in Denmark, for example, parents and children design the curriculum with the help of the teachers. In Scandinavia much of the direction of educational reform is aimed at giving control of the curriculum back to the schools. Schools in Holland are inspected by the Government and assessed according to their own aims and objectives, not by the standard of a centrally prescribed curriculum. Across America there are schools which are designing their own procedures for graduating students. Such autonomy is the critical lever by means of which schools can develop a way of working that is appropriate to their own students, their local communities and the environment. If we are serious about strengthening local communities, empowerment has to begin with education.

In this country the concept of local management of schools has gone a small way towards recognizing that schools should have more autonomy. This initiative, however, only relates to the management of finance enabling more effective use of resources, but has not given schools the independence which they need in order to bring about significant educational changes. It is only by giving teachers and schools autonomy in curriculum areas that our schools will be able to develop educational methods and approaches which are appropriate to our rapidly changing world.

EDUCATION FOR WORK

Thirdly, if education is to prepare young people for meaningful work, the learning process must take account of the way in which the nature of work is changing. The days of a job for life and the security which it brought are over. People therefore need to be much more flexible so that they can change their career path. The management guru, Charles Handy,[8] has suggested that adults should develop a portfolio of skills so that they are able to work in a range of jobs and have the flexibility to respond to the vagaries of the job market. Jobs themselves will continue to change as a result of technological development and so perhaps the skill needed most of all is to know how to learn so that we are able to cope with and adapt to change. An approach to learning which helps young people to become independent learners is therefore far more valuable than one in which they are dependent on teachers telling them what to do.

Employers bemoan the fact that schools are not turning out young people with the skills and attitudes they require and this is further evidence of the need for a different approach to learning. An approach which seeks to develop the whole person and which encourages young people to take responsibility for their lives would over time have a significant impact on the world of work.

A likely and desirable outcome is that young people would become more ethically motivated, which would affect not only how they do their jobs but also which jobs they are prepared to do. This is of central importance in the drive to create a more sustainable world.

SMALLER STRUCTURES

So, if education is about creating a more sustainable world, motivating the child to learn, empowering the child to take responsibility for decisions and enabling him or her to find meaningful employment, learning needs to be organized in a way that will make all of this possible. Smaller structures are the key because they provide an environment in which children can become actively involved in what they are doing. They facilitate the kind of interpersonal relationships which help the child to develop as a balanced person by fostering moral and emotional growth alongside the development of intellectual potential. They allow teachers to respond to children as individuals.

Smaller structures enable schools to create a sense of community. It is only if people feel part of something, as if they belong to it, that they want to participate fully in it. How can a child feel a sense of belonging in a 1000-strong institution where it is not possible even to know the names of all the other people there? When people feel part of a community they have a commitment to making it work. By coming to know the others in their school community and establishing relationships built on trust and openness, young people feel supported and secure. This in turn enables them to build up the self-confidence and self-esteem that are preconditions for learning. Many of the problems in large institutions are a direct result of the superficial relationships that pervade them. If young people are drawn into real relationships they see teachers as people rather than as authority figures and this affects their whole attitude towards school.

Relationships are of critical importance. One often hears it said that someone was inspired by one particular teacher or adult and that this experience was a defining factor in their lives. School must seek to maximize the possibility of such experiences and this can only be done by placing relationships at the centre of the organization.

Smaller structures also make it possible for schools to develop a live relationship with their local community. The community can be a resource for the school, just as the school must be a resource for the local community. Historically schools have taken responsibility for the education of the young and this has left parents and other adults without a significant role. It is clear, however, that this is no longer working and government is trying to shift responsibility for education back to parents and the community.

Schools can play a pivotal role in encouraging pupils to develop a sense of responsibility to their community and vice versa by setting up locally-based project work, work experience and community involvement. Such experiences help young people to develop their own values and shape their lives. And as Colin Ward has said:

> *'every step we make to take children out of the ghetto of childhood into a sharing of interests and activities with those of the adult world, is a step towards a more habitable environment for our fellow citizens, young or old.'*[9]

St Paul's Community School in Balsall Heath, Birmingham, is an example of how a school can be an integral part of a drive to regenerate an inner-city community. It was set up in the 1970s at a time when most other organizations in the area were closing down. It was conceived not as an ordinary school but as a social action experiment working alongside other agencies to improve the community. It is now part of a wider community project which includes a recycling scheme, a community centre, a nursery, financial services for voluntary groups, clubs and classes for local schools. Balsall Heath is now a vibrant and thriving multicultural community in which the school plays a significant role.

Large structures make it very difficult for schools to interact positively and imaginatively with their local community because they lack the flexibility that is required.

Little research has been done in the UK into the benefits of smaller classes and smaller schools, probably because politicians are frightened of the cost implications. There is, however, a growing body of research in the US which indicates the effectiveness of smaller structures in education. This research, which has been collated by Kathleen Cotton,[10] finds that *'small schools do a better job than large ones on virtually every measure of student attitudes and achievement. Teachers like them and their curricula don't suffer.'* Cotton goes on to claim that *'they don't even cost more, it turns out'*. This finding will come as a surprise to many, but is explained by the cost of maintaining a large school infrastructure.

This, and other research into class size, is the driving force behind radical reforms in the US at present. Throughout the state of Tennessee, for example, all infant classes are to be reduced to a maximum size of 20 pupils by the year 2000. At the last count, 26 other states were seriously considering introducing legislation to reduce infant class sizes to 20 and in some cases 15. The state of California is paying schools a significant subsidy if they succeed in reducing infant classes to this level. The Tennessee state government expects to offset the immediate additional costs over time in higher taxes from a better-educated population. In cities across the US large schools are being restructured into schools-within-schools. In Massachusetts, as well as in a number of other states, new autonomous schools, called charter schools, are being set up by community groups and teachers, bypassing state bureaucracy. An article in the *Boston Globe* stated that *'parents across Massachusetts are so hungry for a different type of education for their children that they are swamping the state's charter schools with applications.'*[11]

The Coalition of Essential Schools, a high school/university partnership based at Brown University, which aims to redesign the American High School for better student learning and achievement, recognizes human scale as a necessary precondition for effective learning. Hundreds of schools across America have signed up to the radical agenda set by the Coalition which, among other things, recommends that secondary school teachers have a load of no more than 80 students, that the number of staff in a school should not exceed 25 – 30, that each child and his or her family must be known well by more than one member of staff and that teachers should be generalists first and specialists second. The purpose of these principles is to create learning communities in which the focus is on constructive relationships based on trust. One way in which the Coalition has overcome the problem of large school buildings has been to encourage large schools to restructure into smaller, autonomous units on the same site. The Urban Academy in New York, referred to at the beginning of this chapter, is one such unit.

But the path of such radical reform is not easy and, as Theodore Sizer, the Chair of the Coalition of Essential Schools, comments:

'We are sobered by how hard it is to accomplish change (but) are encouraged by the qualities emerging in the students at those schools which have successfully done so.'[12]

In the UK, Human Scale Education has been committed to a similar set of principles for over ten years, but is finding it difficult to gain a foothold and encourage schools within the state education system to go down this road. A project to encourage large schools to find ways of reorganizing into smaller units in order to give young people a more personal experience of education has found a few schools prepared to consider some degree of restructuring and this has contributed to making education a more positive experience for their young people. There is little doubt, however, that the constraints of the National Curriculum make it very difficult for schools in this country to experiment to find new and better ways of meeting the varying needs of their students.

Human Scale Education was set up to promote smaller structures in education – smaller schools and smaller classes – in the belief that they facilitate *'education as if people matter'*.[13] The membership consists of parents, teachers and, increasingly, professors of education, all of whom are concerned at the inability of the education system to respond to the needs of growing numbers of children. Many of these people are aware of the profound reconstruction which is required in order to create an appropriate education system in our fast-changing world. The organization is contacted daily by parents looking for a school where their children will be happy, by teachers wanting to work in a more humane environment and by community groups wishing to set up a small school or learning centre in their locality. It offers support and advice to all of these people whilst also researching and publicizing examples of good human-scale practice, lobbying government on the issue of size and pressing for public funding for new educational initiatives.

DIVERSITY

Smaller structures are, however, just the beginning. In addition we need dialogue, experimentation and the recognition that there is not one best system. A variegated educational landscape, offering schools with different methodologies and different foci, is far more appropriate to a highly diverse population, with different ways of learning, than a uniform system which seeks to channel all children through the same set of hoops. That so many children are failing to thrive in the present system is in part a direct consequence of this uniformity. As the social entrepreneur Michael Young has said: *'It is because children are not alike, their parents are not alike, their interests are unlike and their needs are unlike that they need different kinds of schools.'*[14]

In a growing number of European countries governments fund different kinds of schools to give parents a real choice about the education which is offered to their children. In Holland for example, Montessori Schools, Rudolf Steiner Schools, Jenaplan schools and faith schools (Christian, Jewish and Muslim) are financed on the same basis as state schools, with the effect that 70 per cent of children attend what are known as 'private' schools, but which are in fact publicly funded. In Denmark any group of 12 parents wishing to set up a school will receive 85 per cent of the necessary funds from the state. The consequence of this is that there is a wide variety of schools within the state-funded system for parents to choose from. Governments in a growing number of European countries, including some former eastern-bloc states, are now realizing that diversity of educational provision is a necessary feature of a pluralist and democratic society and consequently are providing funding for different kinds of schools. Britain is lagging behind in this. Choice and diversity exist, but only for those who are able to pay for it, and this has been and continues to be deeply socially divisive. The most radical reform and the one which would have the biggest impact on educational provision would be to abolish private education as it now exists. By doing this all parents would have a vested interest in improving publicly-funded schools and this would inevitably lead to dramatic improvements to the education system as a whole. An equitable system which provides suitable opportunities for all, rather than one which enables the privileged minority to reinforce their children's already substantial advantage, is surely the way forward to a more just and cohesive society.

The question of whether faith schools should receive state funding is a major issue in the debate about diversity. In January 1998 two Muslim schools became part of the English state system amidst much media coverage and public discussion. As a human rights issue, the decision to publicly fund these schools was long overdue. In a system which finances Protestant, Catholic and some

Jewish schools, it is essential that Muslim schools are funded too, if there is sufficient parental demand, as a matter of justice. Either we should have no religious schools at all (as in France) or give the same rights to different groups of parents, as long as they fulfil the required criteria for state funding which these Muslim schools have done. Muslim and other new faith schools will continue to exist whether or not they receive state funding. It is surely preferable from the children's standpoint that they are part of the system rather than outside it and are thus subject to inspection and required to meet certain standards.

Parents who are given choice are far more likely to feel positively about their child's school, and to work cooperatively with it to support their child's learning. This is crucial in the drive to raise educational standards. Education has to be a true partnership between home and school and this means far more than parents providing somewhere for children to work and overseeing homework. They must have a commitment to what the school is trying to achieve and how it is trying to achieve it, to be able to give their child meaningful support. This can only begin to come about if parents have chosen the school to reflect their own aspirations for their child and thus have an understanding of the school's ethos and methods.

Furthermore the open encouragement of different kinds of schools and different types of learning promotes a dialogue in education. As society changes, schools also must develop both to shape and respond to those changes. A system unprepared to experiment and to learn from those experiments is destined to become obsolete.

This point is emphasised by David Hargreaves, Professor of Education at the University of Cambridge:

> 'The traditional education system must be replaced by poly-morphic educational provision – an infinite variety of multiple forms of teaching and learning. Future generations will look back on our current sharp disjunction between life and education and our confusion of education with schooling as a barrier blocking a – perhaps the – road to the learning society.'[15]

Hargreaves believes that the comprehensive school is in decline. This does not mean the end of the comprehensive principle, but that it can be realized in a variety of ways.

New educational initiatives are being established all the time. Parent/teacher-run schools, community education centres, learning centres for disaffected children and family learning cooperatives all represent a response, usually by parents and local communities, to the shortcomings of an inflexible and outdated system. But currently in the UK they receive no government funding whatsoever, which makes it difficult for them to exist, let alone to thrive. As the vanguard of a new educational era they should be supported and encouraged.

In the short term, smaller structures and a diversity of provision will inevitably cost more. But the long-term costs of not redesigning the education system so that it can meet the needs of all children are far greater. We are already seeing these costs in terms of youth crime, school exclusions, vandalism of school buildings and the continuing exodus of highly skilled, but disaffected, teachers from the profession.

The role of government in education is to raise and distribute money to schools and to inspect schools to make sure that each is achieving what it has set out to achieve. Government has a further responsibility to safeguard the rights of disadvantaged children. Over and above this it should leave the running of schools to the professionals, the local community and the families involved.

That education should be funded from the public purse is not in question. Publicly funded education is an essential tenet of a democratic society and guarantees the independence of schools. Examples of private companies funding schools, in the US in particular – even in the name of innovation – have led to that independence being severely compromised.

CONCLUSION

To create a more sustainable world, schools need to produce questioning, responsible and compassionate people. They must provide the kind of experiences which will help young people to develop a strong moral sense so that they will look critically at what is going on in the world around them and, in the face of huge pressures from the media in particular, have the strength to act according to their convictions. And they must foster in young people the skills and analytical abilities to find solutions to the social and environmental problems which we face.

Regeneration can only come from the grass roots and the challenge for education is to lock into this process to help create strong local democracies within a globalized system. It is only by encouraging and empowering parents and local communities to take responsibility for the education of their children that we will begin to see the variety of schools and educational experiences which are required to meet the very diverse needs of children. It requires a huge shift, but without this shift it is highly unlikely that schools will be able to equip young people to face the main challenge of the next millennium – to create a positive and sustainable future. At Human Scale Education we offer all the help we can to those parents, children and teachers who wish to create more responsive educational communities in which people learn together – and practise sustainability as well as preach it.

REFERENCES

1 Wilkinson, C (1996) 'The Dropout Society: Young People on the Margin', *Young Minds Magazine*
2 Meighan, R (1997) *The Next Learning System*, Nottingham: Educational Heretics Press
3 Tickell, C (1996) 'Education for Sustainability', *Freeing Education* (eds Carnie, F, Large, M and Tasker, M), Stroud: Hawthorn Press
4 Orr, D (1994) *Earth in Mind*, Washington: Island Press
5 Huckle, J and Sterling, S (eds) (1996) *Education for Sustainability*, London: Earthscan
6 Gatto, John Taylor (1992) *Dumbing us Down*, Philadelphia: New Society
7 Gardner, H (1993) *Multiple Intelligences: The Theory in Practice*, New York: Basic Books
8 Handy, C (1995) *The Empty Raincoat*, London: Hutchinson
9 Ward, C (1979) 'Using the Environment in my Teaching', *Talking Schools* (1995) London: Freedom Press
10 Cotton, K (1996) 'School size, school climate and student performance', *Close Up*, no 20, Oregon
11 *Boston Globe*, March 26 1995
12 Sizer, TR (1996) *Horace's Hope*, Boston: Houghton Mifflin
13 Schumacher, EF (1974) *Small is Beautiful*, London: Abacus

14 Young, M (1988) 'Choice in Education', *Resurgence* no 130, Hartland, Devon
15 Hargreaves, DH (1997) 'A Road to the Learning Society', *School Leadership and Management*, vol 17, no 1

3 EDUCATION FOR PARTICIPATION: ART AND THE BUILT ENVIRONMENT

Eileen Adams

Art and the Built Environment was a Schools Council project directed by Colin Ward in the 1970s. It was concerned with the aesthetic and design aspects of environmental study, focusing on the experience of townscape. The project was initially developed at a time when ideas of child-centred learning, social justice and participative democracy permeated educational thinking. What is the relevance of the *Art and the Built Environment* Project today?

One of Ward's principal concerns has been the relationship between people and place.[1] In his foreword to *The Child in the City*, he explains that the book is an attempt to explore the relationship between children and their urban environment.[2] So, too, was *Art and the Built Environment*, a curriculum development project in schools, initially directed by Ward, which aimed to help children develop a sense of place.[3] It sought to promote in them a critical stance to their surroundings, so that they were able to make value judgements about aesthetic and design qualities. As the work developed, it led to involvement in design studies, encouraging young people to consider how we shape the environment and to participate in dealing with change.

The ideas generated through this work have influenced art, design and environmental education in schools in the UK and abroad and are currently being reworked in initial teacher education. Ward described the project as *'a lever of educational change'* and *'a vehicle for the empowerment of the child'*.[4] What is its relevance today?

Today, the context has changed almost beyond recognition. Children are being increasingly denied access to the outdoors. Playing in the street or 'down the rec' or just 'hanging around' in the neighbourhood are no longer options for children. Parents and children are increasingly worried about issues of personal safety for young people, whether the perceived threat is of street crime, drugs, abduction or traffic hazards. Children are increasingly under the supervision and control of adults. When they do spend time by themselves or with other children, it is in front of the television or computer.

While child-centred learning has been under attack from Conservative and Labour governments and the dismantling of both the education and the health services has brought into question the meaning of social justice, the notion of participation has taken on a new lease of life with the advent of New Labour, the new Millennium, Local Agenda 21 and the need for a sustainable future. This brings into sharp focus people's relationship with the environment and the need to deal with the process of change. However, environmental education now seems to be merely an optional extra in the National Curriculum, and where it does exist, the emphasis is on green issues and environmental problems, rather than on urban or cultural concerns which enable young people to explore how we live in towns and cities, to understand how we shape human habitats and how they shape us.

BACKGROUND

Following the publication of the Skeffington Report,[5] the Education Unit at the Town and Country Planning Association was set up in 1970, with Colin Ward as Director. A key concern was to help young people participate in planning issues. In the book *Streetwork: the exploding school*[6] Ward and Fyson set out the rationale for environmental education which underpinned the *Bulletin of Environmental Education* (BEE), the magazine in which Ward was able to speak directly to teachers and pupils about his ideas on society, on citizenship and about participation. Through BEE, his lectures and his involvement in courses for teachers, Ward influenced a generation of teachers, architects and planners, establishing urban environmental education as an exciting, important and challenging area of study.

ART AND THE BUILT ENVIRONMENT

The *Art and the Built Environment* project was initiated by the Art Committee of the Schools Council and based at the TCPA. The challenge for teachers was how to help young people make sense of their experience of the environment, to learn to think and to feel in response to it and to value it and to consider how to deal with the process of change. Art was used as a means of study. The basis was direct experience of the environment. Ward pointed to a continuous line of educational philosophers from Plato to Rousseau, through Schiller, Ruskin and Morris down to Herbert Read, who have urged that education of the senses should be a central task of teachers instead of an optional extra. In *Art and the Built Environment*, the role of the teacher was not so much the expert who knew the answers, but that of guide and mentor who knew the questions to ask. The emphasis was not so much on the knowledge to be transmitted, absorbed and regurgitated, as on the experience to be shared and the meanings which might be generated.

The work developed from a project in a single school[7] to work in ten trial schools in England and Wales,[8] then through a programme of in-service training for teachers, to hundreds of schools in the UK and abroad. It was promoted through the medium of interprofessional working parties, where teachers, architects and planners worked together to influence what was taught in schools.[9] Environmental designers brought a critical dimension to the work and a concern for design, areas where teachers lacked confidence.

SENSE OF PLACE

People are not as negative or as ignorant about architecture and the built environment as the media would have us believe. They are interested in what the environment looks like, what it feels like and are concerned about what it means to them. They can say what draws them to a place or what makes them sick of the sight of it. They might not have heard of the term 'topophilia', but they know what it means. Some of the most popular issues of BEE[10] were those devoted to methods for analysing and appraising townscape quality, initially drawing on Keith Wheeler's work on town trails,

Jeff Bishop's ideas on building analysis and the approaches developed by Brian Goodey and Walter Menzies to townscape appraisal, techniques from geography and architecture which extended established art-based approaches for exploring, observing, recording, analysing and appraising relationships between structures, spaces and people.

To remind them that children's experiences and perceptions of the environment are very different from those of adults, teachers were introduced to the work of environmental psychologists such as Kevin Lynch and David Uzzell. The emphasis on formal qualities of townscape balanced the emphasis elsewhere in the curriculum on science and technology and the socio-political aspects of environmental study. Without such a perception, the environment comes to represent only utilitarian values and neglects the aesthetic and the spiritual.

CRITICAL STUDY

A key consideration was how to develop critical skills in relation to environmental critique. The work of architectural interpreters and critics such as Gordon Cullen, Grady Clay and Ian Nairn was used to help teachers and their pupils develop an appropriate vocabulary for describing townscape experience and to create frameworks for analysis and appraisal. Reference to the history of architecture was not made in terms of the historical development of style, nor was planning approached merely from a socio-economic-political perspective. Rather, Ward attempted to trace some of the aesthetic and design ideas, indicating their origins and the influences which were apparent. Links were created between art and environmental design. In one issue of BEE he showed how the paintings of Claude and Poussin had influenced the form of the English landscape. He also established connections between drawings by Kate Greenaway in *The 19th Century of Vernacular Architecture*, the designs of Parker and Unwin in *The Garden Cities of the Early 20th Century* and illustrations in *The Essex Design Guide* in the 1970s.[11]

Design Education

Following Ward's retirement from the TCPA, the work developed under the direction of Ken Baynes and Eileen Adams at the Royal College of Art (RCA). It was time to reinvest what had been learnt from Baynes' work on the *Design in General Education* Project, established in the RCA in 1970. Key questions were how might young people be helped to deal positively and creatively with the experience of environmental change and how might they influence the design of the environment in the future?

Design requires speculative thinking, where young people develop the skills for hypothesis, supposition and imaginative projection, where they are able to consider alternatives or future possibilities. Imagination is used to confront and create reality. Invention and innovation are the results of creative thinking. Fancy and fantasy have a place, not as an escape but as a means of coming to grips with the world, of making it and creating it anew.

> '*Design is essentially speculative and propositional. It is about the future. All its methods and procedures are directed towards deciding how places, products and images will be. In this respect, it is highly unusual in a curriculum dealing primarily with the past and what we already know. Design is not only knowing about the future, it is about imagining it, shaping it and bringing it about. This needs to be emphasized and made real in learning*'.[12]

Thus the work created a spectrum of study activities which linked people and place. Art work encouraged a personal and emotional response to place. Education for democracy and citizenship was no longer learning about civics, but was to be through active involvement in planning issues and participation in the process of change. All this was already acknowledged:

> '*Environmental education and the exercise of citizenship go hand in hand: the opening-up of opportunities for public participation in decision-making is the most important of all means to environmental education, which should aim at developing a critical, moral and aesthetic awareness of our surroundings*'.[13]

FRONT DOOR PROJECT

The initial project which brought teachers and environmental designers into a working partnership to develop art-based environmental study was the *Front Door* Project at Pimlico School, a comprehensive school in London. A programme of architecture and design studies was developed for all age groups, based on investigation of the local neighbourhood. Eleven-year-olds studied how the area had changed since Victorian times, comparing the 19th century development with the area during the war and the new building afterwards. Twelve-year-olds concentrated on sensory qualities of the floorscape, the quality of Victorian design based on natural form and the experience of pattern based on repetition of a single unit. Thirteen-year-olds explored the notion of change, considering shop fronts as 'soft' architecture, more likely to change than other aspects of the built environment.

Fourteen-year-olds made slide programmes about housing, children's play areas, shop display and shop design. A slide programme on shopkeepers as designers was the inspiration for the first programme in a television series, 'Design Matters', for Channel 4. Young people's perceptions were used as a focus for adult learning. Older pupils chose as their subjects for study from the wealth of architectural gems in the local area: the nineteenth-century housing by Thomas Cubitt and the charitable trusts; Arts and Crafts council housing behind the Tate Gallery; Churchill Gardens Estate and infill developments of the 1950s; and the Lillington Gardens Estate from the 1970s. All the pupils explored relationships between people and place.

LEARNING THROUGH LANDSCAPES

Ideas and techniques from the *Art and the Built Environment* Project were reinvested in a later initiative, *Learning through Landscapes*, which started life as a research project whose aims were to investigate how to extend educational opportunity and how to improve environmental quality in school grounds. The resulting report[14] showed how the school environment could be used as a rich educational resource across the curriculum and how teachers and pupils engaged in experiential and investigative learning activities could make use of the 'outdoor classroom'. This relates closely to the some of the experiments described in Chapter 2, where the school itself becomes one of the major subjects for study and change.

In the last ten years, there has been an explosion of interest in school grounds. Pupils have been observing, recording, analysing and appraising them to identify opportunities or need for change in an attempt to improve environmental quality and extend educational opportunity. At West Walker Primary School in Newcastle, children have helped to plant trees to create a shelter belt. At Hedge End Primary School in Hampshire, pupils have been involved in the development of a nature conservation area, including orchards, where they crop the fruit. At Gillespie Primary School in London, pupils have worked with artists to create play structures and markings for the playground. Pupils in Grangetown Infant School in Cardiff have worked with artists to make murals and seating 'nests'. Pupils at Blackfriars School in Glasgow have built their own pond. These echo the efforts of thousands of children in schools all over the UK.

OPPORTUNITIES

In 25 years the principles have not changed. Education '*in, through*' and '*for*' the environment has become orthodoxy. What has changed is that a new cycle of opportunities has emerged – the National Curriculum, local plans, urban regeneration initiatives, Local Agenda 21, lottery bids, public art projects and school grounds developments. Interprofessional collaboration is seen as a means whereby young people can participate more fully as active citizens in shaping their environment. School grounds offer opportunities where they can put their ideas into action. Local Agenda 21 provides an impetus for them to develop a different view of our relationship with the environment. Changes in the education system point to the need for a reconsideration of the value of direct experience, the importance of the teacher's role and the value of different kinds of learning methods and teaching strategies. With profound changes in the nature of employment and the job market, young people are questioning the purposes of education.

Being able to learn from direct experience will become increasingly significant. The methods developed in *Art and the Built Environment* emphasized the importance of observational, analytical and interpretive techniques. Changes in how learning is managed in schools are bound to have an impact on the role of the teacher. For the moment, teachers in the UK are being reduced to the role of technicians in a service culture that sees education as something to be packaged and delivered. Efforts to limit and constrain the school curriculum will not succeed as knowledge expands and the world becomes more complex. We need to see teachers and learners not as separate and distinct, but as different facets of the same process, linking experience, understanding and action.

INTERPROFESSIONAL COLLABORATION IN EDUCATION

The experience of bringing together different professional groups resulted in curriculum innovation, which could not have been achieved either by teachers or by architects or planners working on their own. The value of the interprofessional working partnerships established was that there was an educational benefit for all participants. Children learnt perceptual, critical, design and communication skills. Art and design teachers developed the confidence and competence to tackle environmental projects. Planners and architects developed techniques which have resurfaced in community architecture and community design initiatives linked with Local Agenda 21. The involvement of environmental designers in education enabled teachers to tackle areas of study previously inaccessible to them. They promoted positive attitudes towards the notion of change and problem-solving, they introduced designerly modes of working, which influenced both the content of studies and the methods employed; they introduced new ideas and vocabulary related to architecture and planning; they shared their expertise in criticism and design, analysing townscape forms and devising strategies for change.

Increasingly, artists are working with schools. With their help, young people have designed sculptures, seats, sundials, railings and gates. Pupils have created temporary and ephemeral pieces on beaches and in forests. They have produced art exhibitions to disturb people into a new consciousness of their environment and their society. They have worked with electronic media and computer-generated images to place communications on the Internet or work with computer-aided design to think about changes to the school environment. Artists often go into schools with the sole purpose of educating young people about art. However, regarding themselves as co-learners – and seeing pupils as artists and designers instead of performers, audience or consumers – would do much to enrich and increase the educational value of such working partnerships. Many current practices in public art[15] would benefit from adopting a similar approach.

EDUCATION FOR SUSTAINABLITY

Messages on sustainability from the Brundtland Declaration have taken a few years to percolate through general consciousness, but just as we were 'sold' the idea in the 1980s that everything was 'country fresh' and 'wholesome', in the nineties everything has to be 'sustainable'. We are aiming for sustainable lifestyles, sustainable futures, sustainable development and education for sustainability. The emphasis tends to be on the use of resources. However, greater equity in the distribution of resources will need greater participation in decision-making regarding how they are used. In *Art and the Built Environment* work, the appearance of towns and cities was seen not only as an indication of our knowledge about materials technology or the development of construction techniques, but as evidence of human choices and decisions of how we choose to live, the result of vested interests, the exercise of power and control. The aim was to help young people develop skills and capabilities so that they could play a part in exercising choice and responsibility and share some of that power and control. This needs to be given a higher profile in environmental education. A convenient label is 'environmental literacy'.

LITERACY

But this is simplistic. 'Literacy' is not about knowing a basic vocabulary and having a rudimentary understanding of language.

It is about dialogue. It is about participating in and contributing to the ideas which shape our society. How these ideas are explored, communicated, shared and shaped is increasingly dependent not merely on words, but on the relationship between words and images. Contrary to popular myth, in the UK we are not visually illiterate. There is a long history and strong tradition of art and design education in schools. The current obsession with design and renewed debate about visual literacy gives a new impetus to the ideas.[16] The concern seems to be, how to develop an understanding of the world of art and design? How to engage with the ideas which artists and designers communicate through their paintings and sculptures, their graphics and furniture, their buildings and land-scapes? The emphasis is on a verbal language to articulate our response.

Art and the Built Environment offered an alternative approach. It extended the focus for visual study to encompass the built environment. It used drawing and photography as conceptual tools for young people to understand the world. Art as a means of *perception* was as important as art as a means of *expression*.

> *'. . . the use of drawing in the project is, in its humble way, a part of the tradition of objective drawing that has its roots in the Renaissance. This has always concerned itself with a humanistic interpretation of the man-made as well as aiding scientific enquiry and providing designers with their most powerful means of shaping what Herbert Read called "the forms of things unknown".'*[17]

As well as using photography and drawing to respond to the world out there, young people used sketches, collages, photomontages, plans, diagrams and constructions with other 'modelling' media to make their ideas visible, to share and shape them, through analysis, reflection and critique. Then they manipulated, reworked, developed and refined their ideas through further work using a battery of techniques and a range of media. Critical study linked visual and spatial 'languages' with words. Both critical study and design activity were seen primarily as group activities, which helped to shape individuals' thinking and develop their skills, through discussion, comparison, debate and argument.

PARTICIPATION

Participation in the design process was seen as a way into participation in the political process. The aim was not only to raise young people's awareness of, interest in and concern about environmental issues. It was to develop the skills so that they could participate more fully in the environmental debate and perhaps influence the political process. One approach has been through *Planning for Real* techniques used in community development, which echoed many of the techniques familiar in schools.[18] These were further developed by environmental and community design organisations such as the Newcastle Architecture Workshop and Community Design for Gwent. Lack of core funding severely curtailed the development of such agencies, but the emergence of new architecture centres, given the blessing of the Arts Council, though not core funding, may create a new focus. Opportunities for participation in planning issues occur frequently, but generally people become involved because they feel threatened by the proposed changes. We have learned only one mode of participation: we have learned to say no; we have perfected the art of objecting.

However, a more positive and creative stance is evident in recent work reported in *Changing Places*.[19] The case studies and working relationships echo themes and methods of working established years ago and reinvest them in new contexts. Angela Eagle, Parliamentary Under-Secretary of State at the Department of Environment, Transport and the Regions, responded:

> '*I am pleased to see an initiative being undertaken that encourages children to view themselves not as consumers, but as stakeholders. By involving them in environmental planning, we provide them with an opportunity both to think about and build the future. Not only is it a chance to consider what they want the environment to be like in the next millennium, it's also a way to develop skills that ensure that, when important decisions are being made, they can make their voices heard and play their part in determining the outcome.*'[20]

WORK ABROAD

The *Art and the Built Environment* project, with its emphasis on the process of learning, provided a model for work in other countries. For instance, ideas and study methods were reinvested in initiatives such as *School Links International,* where children in primary schools in Avon established links with schools in other countries.[21] Each class agreed to study their local environment and to share the results of the work with their partner school. Because all those involved did not speak English, there was a reliance on visual modes of study and communication. Paintings and drawings, maps and plans, slide programmes and video diaries were sent to and fro across the world, so that young children learnt, not only about their own neighbourhood, but also about distant environments.

Courses for teachers, architects and planners in cities as different as Oporto, Vancouver, Adelaide and Sao Paulo adopted similar methods of exploring space and interpreting place. The origin of *Architects in Schools* programmes in the US and other countries lies in the architect-teacher collaborations in Britain in the 1970s. The methods used to develop design education in schools through the *Designwise* programme developed by the National Building Museum in Washington DC were inspired by the work in the UK. The establishment of urban studies (*Stadtstudieren*) and school grounds projects (*Skolans Uterum*) in Sweden was directly influenced by the experience in the UK. Most recently in Japan, *Machizukuri* initiatives, to create greater opportunities for citizen participation in environmental projects, resulted from an exchange programme, where the ideas and techniques generated through work in the UK have been reinvested in other settings such as nature conservation, school grounds and community landscape projects.

CURRICULUM DEVELOPMENT

Through shared evaluation and wider dissemination of the work through a variety of networks, it was possible to promote curriculum development. This was made possible by the existence of the Schools Council, a national government-funded organization for curriculum development. There is no such national focus today.

At a time when the use of computers is creating incredible possibilities for access to information and the communications revolution
is transforming the way we live, the so-called Education Reform
Act and the introduction of the National Curriculum have severely
limited curriculum development and opportunities for teachers to
exercise professional judgement.

At a time of unprecedented change, the school curriculum
cannot be left to stagnate. The model provided by *Art and the Built
Environment* has relevance today. The time is right for new professional collaborations which link art, design and environmental
education. The need is for a national focus and government support
for the necessary research and development.

A new research initiative is being developed involving a
number of centres for initial teacher training. This initiative, linked
with school-based training, offers the opportunity of a collaboration
between pupils, student artist/teachers and teachers similar to
that previously obtaining between teachers and environmental
designers. The teachers bring to it their experience of work in
schools, the pupils bring a knowledge of the local area and students
bring recent experience of their training in art schools and perhaps
their professional experience as artists and designers. In summing
up the significance of this kind of approach and the implications
for research, Bruce Archer explained:

> '. . . one works best from practice towards theory and not the
> other way round; that one works best from the classroom to
> the seminar room and not the other way round; that one best
> works from the teacher to the investigator and not the other
> way round; that one seeks leadership from the field rather than
> from the centre; that action must precede speculation; and
> that it is from the particular that we can arrive at the general
> and not the other way round'.[22]

LEVER OF EDUCATIONAL CHANGE

This advice has particular relevance today. Educational change has
been brought about in the last ten years through political action to
impose managerial practices on schools so that teachers have been
distracted by league tables, targets and testing. Ofsted inspections

have created another form of bureaucratic control. Teachers do not go on courses concerned with learning and teaching, but opt for stress-management instead. With tick lists of competencies to be achieved and hit lists of schools to be improved, in England and Wales at least, teachers' professional confidence has been systematically eroded. Planning, monitoring, assessment and attendance at meetings can take up more of the teacher's time than teaching itself. The education agenda has focused on the management of schools rather than on the quality of the learning and teaching experience.

It is evident that political diktat, examinations and the inspection system are powerful influences on what is taught in schools. However, it is also clear that to be sustainable, good practice needs to be based on sound educational principles and requires the expertise and commitment of good teachers. Good educational practice can be developed only if the link between research and development is placed firmly in the hands of the practitioners, supported by critical friends from other professional groups.

VEHICLE FOR THE EMPOWERMENT OF THE CHILD

Environmental education is presented in schools as issues to be addressed and problems to be solved. However, the answers are not to be found in more science or improved technology. They are to be sought in the strategies we adopt to shape and control our environment and in the consideration of the cultural practices and ethical issues of how we choose to live. It is not enough for children to be aware of environmental issues. It is not enough for them to understand the problems. They need to develop the skills and capabilities to enable them to play a part in shaping their environment.

> *'We are groping for a different political theory . . . The missing political element is the politics of participation . . . environmental education has to be an education that will enable people to become masters of their own environment'.*[23]

Roger Hart, an environmental psychologist, whose work for UNESCO has shown him to be a powerful advocate for children, points to the various forces which are destroying a sense of community and which work against democratic participation as part of daily life.[24] He suggests a kind of 'cultural resistance' to combat the forces of globalism and consumerism to achieve local sustainable development. He sees schools as unlikely settings for this to happen, and points to the value of community environmental centres, which could take on the mission of education for participation. These have much in common with the idea of local environment resource centres which emerged from research into urban study centres in the UK.[25]

By working in collaboration with schools, engaging young people as active learners, bringing together education, environment and design professionals in a working partnership, linking schools with other agencies and organizations in the community, such centres could form an exciting focus and impetus for environmental education. Schools are good at teaching history, helping children learn about the past and what we already know. Environment centres would enable them to look to the future:

> *'Children have an idealism that can generate creative, forward looking solutions to problems: a culture of what could be done in the future rather than what cannot be done because of the past'.*[26]

LOCAL DEMOCRACY AND COMMUNITY LEADERSHIP

The Government is currently asking what we can do to modernize local government through addressing issues of local democracy and community leadership. A recent consultative paper, *Modernising Local Government*, written by John Prescott, the Deputy Prime Minister and Secretary of State for the Environment, Transport and the Regions, asks how to bring government back to the people to create democratic renewal. He talks of people developing *'a vision for their locality . . . to protecting the environment, to developing centres of excellence for the arts and recreation, to revitalising town centres'*. He asks *'for advice on developing new ways in which councils can listen to their communities and involve local people in their decisions and in their policy planning and review'*. He acknowledges that *'There may be value in authorities regularly reviewing and setting out their strategy for consultation and public participation'.*[27]

People do not participate just because they have opportunities to do so, as can be seen in the low turn out at local elections. They do not suddenly start participating in local democracy when they are 18. They need to be interested in their communities, motivated to participate and have the knowledge and skills to do so. They need to feel that they can influence the system. There can be no effective participation without appropriate education, and a fresh look at the *Art and the Built Environment* project might prove invaluable as the starting point for a new generation of environmental education, which we can only assume the new government is keen to see.

REFERENCES

1 Ward, C (1995) *Talking Schools, ten lectures by Colin Ward*, London: Freedom Press
2 Ward, C (1978) *The Child in the City*, London: Architectural Press
3 Adams, E and Ward, C (1982) *Art and the Built Environment: A Teacher's Approach*, Harlow: Longman
4 Ward, C (1995) op cit, note 1
5 Skeffington, F (1969), known as the 'Skeffington Report' but more properly entitled: *People and Planning*, London: HMSO
6 Ward, C and Fyson, A (1973) *Streetwork: the Exploding School*, London: Routledge
7 Harahan, J (1976) *Eight Projects in Design Education*, London: The Design Council
8 Adams, E and Ward, C (1982) op cit, note 3
9 Adams, E (1982) *Art and the Built Environment: Working Parties*, York: Longman Resources Unit
10 TCPA (1976-9) *Bulletin of Environmental Education*
11 *A Design Guide for Residential Areas*, Essex County Council, 1973
12 Baynes, K (1982) *Beyond Design*, unpublished paper
13 UN (1970) 'Final Report of the International Working Meeting on Environmental Education on the School Curriculum'
14 Adams, E (1990) *Learning through Landscapes: the Design, Use, Management and Development of School Grounds*, Winchester: Learning through Landscapes Trust

15 Adams, E (1997) 'Public Art and Work in Schools', *Journal of Art and Design*, National Society for Education in Art and Design

16 Raney, K (1997) *Visual Literacy:Issues and Debates*, Middlesex University School of Education

17 Baynes, K (1982) *Design Studies*, vol 3, no 4, October

18 Gibson, T (1993) *Making it Happen: A User's Guide to the Neighbourhood Action Packs*, Lightmoor

19 Adams, E and Ingham, S (1998) *Changing Places: Young People's Participation in Environmental Planning*, London: The Children's Society

20 Ibid

21 Beddis, R and Mares, C (1988) *School Links International*, WWF and Avon Local Education Authority

22 Archer, B (1976) *On from the Art and the Built Environment Project*, paper at the ABE Summer School, July, Royal College of Art, London

23 Ward, C (1995) op cit, note 1

24 Hart, R (1997) *Children's Participation, The Theory and Practice of Involving Young Citizens in Community Development and Environmental Care*, London: Earthscan

25 Kean, J and Adams, E (1991) *Local Environmental Resources Centres*, Newcastle Architecture Workshop

26 The Children's Society (1998) *Children's Planning and Environment Month*, February

27 Prescott, J (1998) *Modernising local government. Local Democracy and Community Leadership*. Department of the Environment, Transport and the Regions

FURTHER READING

Adams, E (1997) *Public Art: People, Projects, Process*, Sunderland: AN Publications

Bishop, J, Adams, E and Kean, J (1992) *Children, Environment and Education: Personal Views of Urban Environmental Education in Britain*, Children's Environments, vol 9, no 1

Clay, G (1973) *Close-Up: How to Read the American City*, Praeger

Cullen, G (1971) *The Concise Townscape*, Architectural Press

Lynch, K (1960) *The Image of the City*, MIT Press

Moore, R (1990) *Childhood's Domain: Play and Place in Child Development*, MIG Communications
Slafer, A and Cahill, K (1995) *Why Design? Activities and Projects from the National Building Museum*, Chicago Review Press, p 56

PART III

A Roof Over Your Head

4 LOOKING FORWARD AND LOOKING BACK: STATE PROVISION AND SELF-HELP IN HOUSING POLICY

Alison Ravetz

It says much for today's society that the most salient housing issue is not the homeless on our streets, nor even the thousands of home 'owners' who are suffering the misery of building society repossession. Rather, it is where to place the four-and-a-half-million new homes that are needed for the expected increase in households over the next 20 years, and the resistance of those living near any earmarked sites to this intrusion into their space. Housing had no profile in the landslide Labour victory of 1997, a far cry indeed from that other landslide in 1945, when – and for a series of elections following – housing was the burning issue. Yet sometimes it seems as if the conventional wisdom of housing has moved remarkably little since those times. Opposing it is a small, but persistent anarchist vision, owed very largely to the writings of Colin Ward; but even this in its way is rooted in the conventional debate. The question that exercises me here is how far either debate, the conventional or the unconventional, really addresses the challenges of the future. Might it be that in housing questions, as in other aspects of public welfare, we are in something of an ideological vacuum?

A QUESTION OF TENURE?

The mainstream housing debate is conducted in terms of public sector versus the market. The anarchist perspective, on the other hand, sees housing as an arena of individual versus the state – the state in this case represented by council housing (as I shall call it here, although officially the term is now replaced by 'social housing', to include the voluntary sector). The mainstream debate has always been dominated by tenure: in particular the relative privilege of home-owning and renting. In an obvious sense this is an important dichotomy as it has been so prominent in housing policy, but in another respect it is unhelpful, because it obscures the extent to which our system is a hybrid one, a fusion of market and welfare, where tenure distinctions are not always the most crucial ones.

It can also be misleading in that it leaves out the historical dimension. It is true that at various times the age of the housing stock has been a major concern – notably about 30 years ago, when clearance programmes were dedicated to progressive replacement of older dwellings. The lack of historical appreciation is of a more subtle kind than this: failing to appreciate the cumulative nature of housing (stock, tenures, attitudes and expectations) has amounted to a failure to appreciate the historical uniqueness of any particular conjunction of these things. It is not so much that we take for granted what we have inherited from the past, as that we fail to see what parts of the present system are merely 'coasting', perhaps for a very limited remaining period. This then restricts our grasp of options for the future – our ideas, so to speak, could also be coasting on inherited attitudes.

Even before the state actively intervened in housing there was a crucial affordability gap between the less affluent and the cost of a roof. The gap became acute with the imposition of sanitary and overcrowding standards from the 1870s onwards and, one way or another, all housing policy since has been concerned with bridging or somehow reconciling this gap for ever-growing numbers. It was the initial reason behind subsidies for council housing and, less obviously, it was the motive of the other type of subsidy given, the fiscal one. This has taken different forms at different times, even falling under different departments of government for renters and home owners; but the purpose has always been to make what society deemed to be decent housing available to ever-larger populations.

Concentration on the renting:owning polarity has tended to conceal numerous layers of privilege within, as well as between, tenures. It is not the case, as popular opinion often assumes, that renters are invariably exploited by having to pay rent at all – now that home ownership is so common, the argument goes that rent is 'wasted money' which could otherwise go towards buying a house. The reality is that since 1915, when an emergency rent freeze was imposed on private landlords, the great majority of tenants have not paid an economic rent for their homes. For decades tenants of private landlords paid frozen or only partially unfrozen rents (with lasting consequences for the upkeep of the stock) while council, and later housing association, rents were kept down by the bricks-and-mortar subsidy for building.

PARITY OF ESTEEM?

Without all these various subsidies, 20th century Britain would never have achieved its present housing standards and here is an area of relative privilege that is often overlooked. For many years it has been taken as axiomatic that houses built by private developers for owner-occupation are superior to those built by local authorities for their tenants – a view that reflects the low esteem into which council housing has fallen, exacerbated by the disastrous experiment of high-rise flats in the 1950s and 1960s, and reinforced by the policy of tenant 'right to buy' which creamed off much of its best stock in the 1980s. The perception is not, however, strictly true to the historical record. The earliest council houses set trail-blazing standards for working-class housing, although these were later compromised by economies and overtaken in a number of technical respects by the speculative house-builders of the 1930s. In 1945, however, the public sector took a clear lead, building to standards that, within given price bands, were never surpassed by private developers, who later emulated them. They were never, however, obliged to follow the Parker Morris standards required in all public and social housing from 1969 to 1981 and which, despite various limitations, have since set new levels of space and internal fittings in public housing.

These points do of course contradict popular perceptions of council housing, which are coloured by the appalling conditions now found on problem estates: not only the notorious high-rise flats hurriedly erected and dismantled, in many cases with scarcely half their loan-repayment period expired, but the equally problematic walk-up flats and maisonettes and estates of 'Radburn' layout, with huge amounts of useless space that is neither public nor private. Yet for many decades British council housing was the cynosure of visiting professionals from overseas, who admired its internal fittings and high space standards – something that seems confirmed by the fact that a quarter of all tenants have chosen to buy the homes they rented. The main fault, it appears, was not so much in design as such, but rather in a chronic lack of maintenance (particularly crucial in high flats and all technically innovative buildings) coupled to a lack of – in a literal sense – caretaking. Many estates were also doomed by being built as huge, isolated, one-class districts that are now dominated by unemployment, mass dependency on benefits and criminality.

Here is the nub of the inequalities between council tenants: for while some enjoyed high-quality dwellings and estates, others were in hard-to-let property from which there was no escape. Owner occupation does not show quite such contrasts, although there are considerable differences between the fortunates who have contin-uously improved their status by 'trading up' and those trapped in decaying inner-city districts ravaged or blighted by slum clearance, roadworks or other major planning surgery. Housing privilege, therefore, is more than a matter of renting or owning: it depends very largely on a combination of tenure and quality.

HOUSING THE NUCLEAR FAMILY

The picture is still not complete, however, until we note for whom new housing has habitually been built. The overwhelming prop-ortion of additions to the housing stock has been for those nuclear families with sufficient means and security to pay rent or repay loans. Other categories – extended or abnormally large families, single people, migrants, immigrants and the poor in general – have traditionally been left to fend for themselves. In the past they were not even expected to have homes of their own, but rather to lodge in the family-homes of others or to find beds in institutions. It was only when slum clearance began in earnest in the 1950s that they 'inherited' a pool of older housing vacated by families moving to council estates or suburbs.This eventually prompted the anti-slum clearance and squatting campaigns, when rolling programmes of clearance threatened to remove humble and substandard, but relatively cheap, housing that offered shelter to people not catered for elsewhere in the system.

Later policy went only a small way to redress the imbalance between family and household types. Housing for elderly people, pioneered before 1939 by progressive councils, was given priority from the 1950s, but it was only with the reconstitution of the Housing Corporation in 1974 that housing associations were funded to house particular categories whose needs were not being met – in practice, single people, ex-offenders and various of society's rejects. But supply never met demand and one of the more extreme consequences of the shortfall is seen in our young homeless street-dwellers who are, quite literally, left out in the cold. While it would be unreasonable to blame past housing policies for economic and social trends that were not foreseen and were never within their scope, it is nevertheless true that their gearing to a broad majority has excluded those on the margins.

Does this then mean that our housing system has failed, or only that it has failed some people? Not surprisingly, since it set out to serve them, the majority are quite contented with the way they are housed. Recent data[1] show that, overall, more than half of all households are 'very satisfied' with their accommodation and only about ten per cent are not satisfied at all. The most contented are the elderly, those owning their homes outright and those living in bungalows or detached houses. The least contented are people living in flats and terraced houses, and tenants of councils and private landlords. There is most dissatisfaction (two-and-a-half-times the average rate) in ethnic minority households.

A PERSONAL RELATIONSHIP WITH THE HOME

It is of course possible to question the true significance of such crude measures. To the extent that the range of choice is limited, asking people for a discriminating answer is about as realistic as asking them how much they like supermarket bread. It is also the case that, through the later 20th century, people have steadily developed a more personal relationship with their homes,[2] and this gives them a strong stake in liking, or at least declaring that they like, the homes they currently have.

But from a still wider perspective than this it would be possible to argue that there are respects in which our housing system has performed quite well, even if by chance rather than design. With a stock that is only augmented by about two per cent or less each year – so that a quarter of all dwellings now existing were built before 1914 – a whole domestic technical revolution has been accommodated. Through a combination of demolition, modernization and new building, electrical supply, hot water systems, fixed baths and internal toilets became virtually universal between 1950 and 1980, with central heating following in about 80 per cent of our homes. Over the same period the stock of dwellings quietly absorbed a veritable explosion of personal possessions including, latterly, a wealth of computers and electronic equipment. Admittedly, this was made easier by the much lower occupancy of houses than in former times, although it was also associated with a striking shrinkage in the envelope of the family house and the virtual disappearance of built-in storage space. It is, therefore, a moot question how far hobbies, serious study, or the spreading pattern of working from home will find room in the pretentious, but tiny, houses now being built. Even 'telecottaging' requires space.

HOUSING POLICY AND THE RESTRUCTURING OF THE MODERN CITY

These are small issues, however, in the face of the looming environmental ones that confront us. Water, energy and fossil fuels will all become increasingly precious, making conservation and conversion to renewable resources urgent in a way not yet real to most people. Housing, which takes up half or more of all urban land, must necessarily be involved in any restructuring of the city, although it is as yet far from clear what should be the model for optimum 'sustainability' in the future. There are arguments both for high-density, compact neighbourhoods with easy access to local resources and dispersed, low-density settlements conducive to horticulture and self-sufficiency. Either way, the scale of change required is daunting for a housing system that has up to now changed only incrementally and more or less accidentally.

For many years a figure of £20 billion has been given as the estimated cost of repairing and modernizing council housing. The stock of owner-occupied houses now presents a similar challenge: it has the same proportion but, because of its size, about four times the amount of unfit dwellings as the public sector. It is hard to imagine from where the necessary investment will come, simply to repair our existing stock of houses, let alone to make them all energy-efficient – not least in view of the often-repeated statement that at today's rate of replacement our existing housing stock will have to serve for the next 500 to 1000 years: as long, that is, as between ourselves and the Armada, if not the Norman Conquest.

It is the case, then, that although a housing system that grew up for an earlier society has served more or less adequately up to now, it will shortly face pressures of an order not experienced before. How far are we prepared, even mentally, to confront those pressures? One obvious thing to do is to look at the measures taken by people to redirect the housing system to their own ends and the ways in which they have actively intervened in the system, rather than keeping to their usual roles of passive consumers and clients. In particular, how far does their example validate the argument, put from an anarchist perspective by Colin Ward and others, that if people could only be freed to do their own thing – to create the housing they really want – then we would have both better housing and a better society?

DO IT YOURSELF HOUSING

The evidence for direct action of this kind is not abundant. In the nature of things it is poorly recorded and lacking in systematic analysis as to its occasions, purposes, costs and replicability; how far it is an individual or a group activity, reactive or proactive, pragmatic or ideological; and most crucially, how far its intent was simply to join the mainstream, or to bring about radically new ways of housing and living. It is hard to gather enough material for any coherent account of our 'alternative' housing history, and we are all in debt to Ward's writings which are often the only accessible source for unpublished projects. There is, it appears, no established canon of practice, but rather a scattered collection of examples showing all the above and still more, with many overlaps, repeats and contradictions.

Squatting, for instance, numerically the most important self-help strategy, extends over the whole spectrum, from individual and furtive use of land and structures, to organized group-takeovers of army camps after both World Wars and the quasi-political movement of the 1960s, which was much influenced by the anti-nuclear campaigns.[3] With a new goal of claiming the right of single people to homes of their own, it now became a form of community action, that had considerable success in halting slum clearance or inhumane planning developments, as in the celebrated 'battle for Tolmers Square'.[4] It also became the vehicle of what squatters claimed was a new urban culture, expressed through festivals, community art and environmental concerns such as recycling and wholefoods. This wave of squatting had a lasting impact on housing policy, influencing the eventual closure of the notorious 'Part 111' hostels for homeless families that came down from the Victorian workhouse, and resulting in the licensing of thousands of squatted properties through new short-life housing associations and cooperatives. In all, some tens of thousands of people were involved and the squatting culture continues to play a part in society today, although with a lower public profile. Its adherents pioneer (as they would see it) new forms of domestic, family and neighbourhood life through their unconventional patterns of work, consumption, food, childcare and personal relationships.

There are other groups that loosely belong to the same culture, but without being urban: the Tipi folk who created their own village in a remote Welsh valley; the New Age travellers whose yearly rhythms are based on festivals and who use the town mainly for winter quarters; and the peace campers and 'eco-warriors' whose benders, tree houses and tunnels are a necessary accompaniment of protests against nuclear missiles and roadworks.

Another intervention that breaks through the conventional housing system is 'self-build'. Astonishingly large numbers are claimed for the contribution of self-building to the housing stock each year, but the great bulk of it is done with no other purpose than to provide owner-occupiers with custom-designed homes on which they save labour costs. Much of it is managed by specialized commercial companies offering a limited range of house designs, and the end result is usually the perennially popular bungalow or detached house. But self-building is also used for radical purposes by individuals and small groups to produce solar or self-sufficient houses, and such variants as the underground or 'earth-sheltered' house. Clearly it then has an ideological as well as practical dimension – indeed, there could hardly be a more anarchist state-ment than a house that is independent of all centralized services.

A similar combination of the practical and the ideological is seen in 'Lewisham Self-build' and its derivatives. This simple prefabricated system was devised by the late Walter Segal to enable inexperienced people to construct their own homes, using small sites that would normally be thought uneconomic to develop. Colin Ward was instrumental in getting a borough council to take it up for people on its waiting list and the result is several small clusters of unique houses, each bearing the imprint of its owner's desires and personality, and the system has spread throughout the country.

In the meantime, Ward was highlighting the significance of the curious phenomenon of the 'plotlands', those areas of farmland mainly in Essex, the SE and Thames valley, where land was sold off in small plots for weekend and holiday use.[5] They first appeared in about 1900, but the main period of growth was between the wars when many of London's east-enders were able to make a down-payment and to build themselves primitive shelters, often from disused buses and railway coaches, which they gradually, and often illicitly, expanded into permanent homes. The 1947 Town and Country Planning Act, with its universal development control, brought all such activity to an end, although planning law had no power to remove existing structures.

What particularly impressed Ward and Hardy, the chroniclers of this movement, was the amount of cooperation and community work involved in the creation of what were, in effect, ad hoc settlements, and their capacity to endure, grow and eventually evolve into permanent ones. Thus Peacehaven on the Sussex cliffs, though savagely criticized by architects and planners, evolved into a small town in its own right. Pitsea and Laindon in Essex, which by 1939 housed about 25,000 people, were eventually absorbed into Basildon New Town. After the publication of *Freedom to Build* in 1972, a parallel was drawn between these spontaneous settlements and the vast squatter- or shanty-town settlements that were by then springing up around every developing-world city.[6]

In the 1970s self-build and the memory of the plotlands were brought together by Ward and others in a movement for a new garden city, which was to be located in the new town of Milton Keynes. The projected 'Greentown' came to grief for many reasons, not least the unwillingness of the planning authority to sanction a mixture of homes and workplaces on the same site. There was more success with Lightmoor on a site within Telford New Town, a 'new community' of the TCPA that took form under the guidance of Tony Gibson and the Neighbourhood Initiatives Foundation. Nine families built houses for their own occupation and they were later joined by five housing association tenants who built their own homes with a Segal-derived system. Although it was intended as the first phase of a much larger project, access to land and other difficulties prevented the hoped-for growth to 400 households.

PARTICIPATION AND DESIGN

Radical self-build thus remained a small minority activity and the fact that its end product was usually owner occupation meant that any distinctive qualities were likely to be confined to its early pioneering phase. Of much wider significance was 'participation in design', for which there have been many more opportunities. With this, people have been able to work in groups on the design (or redesign) of their homes and estates, often with power to commission their own architects and contractors and control their own budgets. This was the stuff of 'community architecture' which rose to prominence in the 1980s, when it owed much to the support of the Prince of Wales and his friendship with Rod Hackney, initiator and architect of the Black Road improvement scheme in Macclesfield, a district of small, pre-Victorian houses that would normally have been demolished. Instead, with General Improvement Area status, the houses were converted and enlarged to the individual specifications of each separate occupant. Land was pooled and reallocated to private or shared uses, space was made for cars and the whole impressively landscaped and planted.

Design participation embraced privately-funded groups like the Great Eastern Association on the Isle of Dogs (some of whose members were also self-builders), but it was most likely to arise from the replacement of demolished council estates whose tenants had won the right to design new houses and layouts, or from housing cooperatives registered with the Housing Corporation. Mostly, such schemes involved no more than 40 households and their plans had to fall within the usual criteria of public funding. Even so, participants often felt able to be more adventurous than local authority architects – for instance with the inclusion of shared open space – and the lavishly planted and well cared-for clusters made a striking contrast with the urban dereliction or abandoned council estates around them. One of the arguments put forward for participation in design is that because it reflects the choices of real individuals it has the ability to deliver 'organic' environments that give the impression of having evolved over long periods of time, but the most cogent argument for it is the sense of enablement and personal fulfilment felt by participants.[7]

HOUSING COOPERATIVES

Classic examples of participatory housing design are found in the housing cooperatives of Liverpool and Coin Street on the south bank of the Thames. Cooperative housing in general, however, is one of the surprising disappointments of British housing. Having been the initiators, first of the mutual building society and then of cooperative trading, one might have expected Britain to take the lead in cooperative housing. But the early building societies developed into mere lending institutions and when cooperative wholesale societies did engage in housing it was either as mortgagors or conventional landlords. Co-partnership housing, associated with the garden city movement in about 1900, did successfully house many thousands before 1914, but after the Great War it was completely eclipsed by the innovation of council housing. So also was the 'voluntary sector' of non-profit housing societies, even though these long predated and were in many ways a precedent for it.

After a shortlived experiment with co-ownership in the 1970s, cooperative housing had to be reimported from Scandinavia (where it had first been inspired by the British cooperative movement!). Under the reformed Housing Corporation of 1974, housing cooperatives received the same generous grants and other treatment as housing associations, although this was not always appropriate for their essentially anarchic structure. Over the next ten years their numbers grew rapidly, with main concentrations in London, the Home Counties and Merseyside. In these mutual or par-value cooperatives, the rising value of the property remained vested in the group – unlike co-ownership, members could not realize any personal gain. The cooperative, as a body, received allowances for self-management, from which it was possible to accumulate annual surpluses over which it had discretion, and it sometimes had access to other funds for such community amenities as club houses for the elderly. Design was often done by members themselves or through the agency of a secondary cooperative. As well as all the technical considerations, this entailed the working out of a group philosophy concerning such points as who should be eligible for membership, how to design entrances and otherwise present the estate to the outside environment, how to divide open space between private and collective use and whether or not to include children's playgrounds. The group philosophy was often extended to a commitment to proselytization and training others in cooperative procedures. Thus the Weller Street housing cooperative of Toxteth in Liverpool, though it did not achieve all it hoped in this respect, did commission and publish a full length book on its experience.[8]

The two most ambitious and successful cooperatives each owed their existence to a unique combination of political circumstances. The Eldonian Village in Vauxhall, Liverpool, on the site of an abandoned sugar refinery, built a larger than usual number of houses, which it linked to local industries and training, health and child care facilities. The Coin Street community builders initiated a whole series of commercial enterprises including craft workshops and markets, as well as a string of housing cooperatives. Both insisted that ordinary family homes should have a place in city centres: but in the case of the Eldonians this was on blighted and disparaged land that people normally shunned for life in the suburbs, while at Coin Street it was land that was valued so highly that it would normally have precluded housing. The projects were alike in that they concerned not only housing, but urban – and indeed social – regeneration, so affirming in the words of the Coin Street logo that 'There is Another Way'.

The question is how to evaluate such a disparate set of examples and, more particularly, to determine how far they provide a pathway into the future. Other than squatting and the plotlands, they have added infinitesimal amounts to the national housing stock, but as Ward maintains, significance does not necessarily depend on numbers. For him, the vital thread between them is user-control over housing, and the important thing is that anarchist solutions should arise regardless of context. If the 'right' context (in anarchist terms) is awaited they will never arise at all. In sum, they show how much ordinary, powerless people have been able to achieve in the face of the state. How much more, then, would be achieved if the state stood aside and let them use their innate ability to house themselves?

THE 'FREEDOM-TO-BUILD' THESIS

The view is buttressed by the *Freedom-to-Build* thesis. The great insight this offered was that the squatter housing created by the poor and powerless of developing countries is not to be judged by official criteria, which it breaches time and again. Its value lies in its aptness for the resources that are actually available to people and its liberating effect on their lives. In effect, it gives them three 'freedoms' that many of the supposedly well-housed have had stripped away: freedom to choose their own communities, budget their own resources and shape their own environments. The outcome has been a level of urbanization that could never be achieved by government fiat. The 'plotlands' were, in Ward's view, Britain's version of developing-world shanty towns, and this inspires him with a vision of the future where the state would sponsor similar schemes, providing only land and infrastructure, as a means of rescuing our inner cities. There would be a *'carnival of construction'* with

> *'long queues of families anxious to build the rest of the house for themselves, or to employ one of our vast number of unemployed building workers to help, or to get their brother-in-law or some moonlighting tradesman . . . Why, it would be like those golden days at Letchworth!'*[9]

This fairly evokes the immense excitement reported on the numerous occasions when housing cooperatives and tenant groups on run-down council estates launched their schemes of renovation or new building – an infinitely precious collective experience that deserves to be repeatedly commemorated. But there are some underlying assumptions here that need closer examination. One is that our inner cities, or some of them, are past redemption through any of the usual channels. For Ward, *'there may be no other way of rescuing inner Liverpool'*.[10] There is of course no doubt that our more desperate situations have prompted some brilliant remedies, but how far there is a universal need for these, or how far they could provide a template for all contexts, is not so clear.

Another assumption is that the shanty-town builders of 'exploding' cities in the developing world are a fair parallel to our own plotlanders; but these were not so much trying to join urban life as escaping from it, to an aptly named 'arcadia'. We may query (as planners and architects did at the time) how far good models are presented by Peacehaven's overall density of one house to the acre and 26 miles of sewers and cables, or by Jaywick Sands, built on a floodplain and engulfed by the disastrous inundation of 1953. It may well be that many Britons today have the same yearnings for freedom as those earlier plotlanders, with less opportunity to satisfy them, but they might well be contented with something more like European garden allotments than licence to build their own towns. Conventional home ownership, as Ward concedes, already provides many with the three essential 'freedoms', or appears to do so. There is little sign that the majority are straining to create their own homes and neighbourhoods: on the contrary, as we have seen, they are somewhat distressingly complacent. Were there, for instance, any widespread desire for housing cooperatives, people could form their own without any 'say-so' from the state.[11]

To compare the currently urbanizing societies with Britain, the first industrialized and urbanized country in history, is not of course to compare like with like. Ours is a society habituated to centralized and bureaucratic government, on which it is very probably too dependent. But would rule by autonomous, self-help groups be superior? The answer is that we do not know. Those groups pursuing 'another way' of creating homes and environments are such a rarity that it is natural to focus on their most innovative and valiant aspects. They are not, however, immune to the common problems of leadership and decision-making, such as the apathy of many, internal divisions, need for training and the danger of an effective leadership becoming a new élite.

The most germane point, however, is that where direct action in housing – user control and DIY settlements, for example – has occurred, it has been in reaction to the established system. Its participants have not, with some partial exceptions, set out to create blueprints for an alternative housing system or policy framework. Much of the action in question has been prompted from the state, at either local or central level, and still more of it has depended on state support. Tenant management cooperatives, for instance, were licensed by an Act of 1975; housing cooperatives and self-build societies were sponsored by the Housing Corporation; the Priority Estate Project and its descendant Estate Action, where council tenants are involved in the regeneration of their estates, were central government initiatives. At the local level we have already noted Lewisham's adoption of the Segal self-build experiment and other notable one-off examples include Newcastle's Byker estate and Hackney's Lea View House, designed and redesigned, respectively, with 'community architecture' consultants. One of the most comprehensive examples is provided by the city of Glasgow, which responded, after the mistakes of its slum clearance and high-rise policies became apparent, by promoting tenement improvement schemes, community-based housing associations and tenant cooperatives, and encouraged the Tenant Participation Advisory Service.[12]

PROVIDERS OR ENABLERS?

The fact is that official policy and direct action have reflected off one another, helped by the several generations of 'graduates' that now exist: men and women who work on either side of the fence in the course of their lives, eventually fanning out into local or central government, professional practice or community and voluntary agencies. Twenty-five years ago there was talk – much of it from Ward himself – of local authorities becoming housing 'enablers' rather than direct providers: a role that was intended to bridge the rigid and unhelpful divides of public and private, renting and owning. Although it is the current fashion to give plaudits to Thatcherism by saying that its reforms were necessary if harsh, I still hold to an opposite view, that its ideology-driven obsession with privatization and determination to erase the public sector was a tragedy for the more considered ideas, reforms and adjustments to policy that were then emerging.

This may now be history, but it is not yet irrelevant. It lands us, in fact, in the midst of the most up-to-date debates on the role of the state, the boundaries of state and individual responsibility, and the function – if any – of the public sector. Cole and Furbey have noted how, of all that the welfare state had to offer, council housing was the 'benefit' most at risk since, unlike health and education, it was not extended to the middle classes.[13] More than this, as it reached down the social scale, it came to carry and so be blamed for problems not dealt with elsewhere in the economy or the body politic. No doubt there is much about council housing that we would, with the benefit of hindsight, do differently. Its simultaneous aims of cheap rents and raised housing standards sat awkwardly together, and its particular tragedy was that, in flagrant contradiction of its first intent, it came to create, as much as bridge, social divides. But it remains a reality of present-day society, still providing over a fifth of the housing stock overall (very much more locally, in many places), and there are many who continue to depend on it. What is more, as society changes and the inadequacies of our housing system become apparent, we see that we need more rather than less housing to rent.

We should be careful, therefore, what target to attack if we wish to orient ourselves to the future rather than the past. While Ward would jettison council housing altogether by whatever means (including the wholesale conversion of tenants into home owners through the right to buy) it would be better to look at the system as a whole rather than discriminating against one part of it. Housing is a collective creation: a stock of physical as well as financial equity. Its building stock constitutes a built environment that in many respects is as constraining and as slow to change as the natural environment. Equally important, if less visible, is its financial equity and perhaps it is here, as much as anywhere, that attitudes need to change. For instance, it is found acceptable for private owners to cash and release their assets into the inheritance chain, while public owners have up to now been debarred from realizing or using the value of their property to create more housing.

The point is that housing is a store of wealth that can generate more wealth, employment and other socially desirable things; but only when we take the broadest view and see it as a collective possession are we likely to come up with a genuinely radical approach to its future. It would of course be folly not to incorporate the energy and achievements we find in direct intervention and self-help in housing (and to this end, one of the most practical things we could do is ensure that they are properly recorded and disseminated). The task for the future remains, as always, how to enable all citizens to attain decent homes. We did not manage this in the past and the problem is now more challenging as it must be done within parameters of what is physically and socially sustainable.

REFERENCES

1 Green, H and Hansbro, J (1995) *Housing in England 1993–4*, OPCS, London: HMSO; Green, H et al (1997) *Housing in England*, ONS, London: HMSO

2 Ravetz, A with Turkington, R (1995) *The Place of Home: English Domestic Environments 1914–2000*, London: Spon.

3 Wates, N and Wolmar, C (eds) (1980) *Squatting: the Real Story*, London: Bayleaf Books

4 Wates, N (1976) *The Battle for Tolmers Square*, London: Routledge & Kegan Paul

5 Hardy, D and Ward, C (1984) *Arcadia for All: the Legacy of a Makeshift Landscape*, London: Mansell

6 Turner, JFC and Fichter, R (eds) (1972) *Freedom to Build: Dweller Control of the Housing Process*, New York: Macmillan

7 Woolley, T (1986) 'Community Architecture: an Assessment of the Case for Participation in Design' in: Scott, J and Jenks, M (eds) *What is the Point of Community Architecture?* Oxford Polytechnic Department of Town Planning, WP 95

8 McDonald, A (1986) *The Weller Way. The Story of the Weller Streets Housing Cooperative.* London: Faber & Faber

9 Ward, C (1990) *Talking Houses. Ten lectures*, London: Freedom Press, p.25 (Note: Letchworth was the first garden city, founded 1903)

10 Ibid, p 34

11 Treanor, D (1987) *Buying Your Home with Other People*, London: Shelter and NFHA

12 Ospina, J (1987) *Housing Ourselves*, London: Shipman

13 Cole, I and Furbey, R (1994) *The Eclipse of Council Housing*, London: Routledge

PART IV

Other Landscapes, Other Ways

5   A PEOPLED LANDSCAPE

Colin Ward

Our perceptions of our surroundings are as subject to changes in fashion as our attitudes to any human artefact. In the early 18th century, when Defoe travelled to Westmorland, he found it *'a country eminent only for being the wildest, most barren and frightful of any that I have passed over in England.'* For it lacked the signs of human activity, ingenuity and well-being that mattered to him. A century later, the Lake poets sanctified that district as a place where, in the words Bishop Heber used for another tourist attraction, *'every prospect pleases, and only man is vile.'*

The paradoxical result of this cult of 'wild' nature combined with misanthropy towards mere humans was that by 1995 it was possible for Jonathan Croall, who writes in Chapter 9, to visit Cumbria and report that *'the sole path up the spine of Helvellyn had gradually been widened by the pressure of walkers, so that it begins to resemble a trunk road.'*[1] Tourism dominates while productive activity declines. Discussing the economic problems of small hill farmers, as opposed to factory farmers, Fay Godwin, a close observer of the rural scene, asks, *'Do we want these lived-in landscapes to become cloned theme-parks regulated by the heritage industry?'* For she argues that

> *'current government thinking will lead not only to further rural depopulation, but also to the loss of many of our most valued landscapes, whose character has been formed by small farmers over thousands of years, unlike the wilderness national park areas in other countries.'*[2]

She is right to stress that ours is a landscape constructed by human activity over centuries. Peter Kropotkin, geographer and anarchist, described how over a century ago he took a knapsack and went on foot out of London, and saw empty fields within ten miles of

Charing Cross in a city supplied with Flemish and Jersey potatoes, French salads and Canadian apples. When he asked why, the explanation was 'Heavy Clay', with no recognition (Kropotkin complained) that

> '. . . in the hands of man there are no infertile soils; that the most fertile soils are not in the prairies of America, nor in the Russian steppes; that they are in the peat-bogs of Ireland, on the sandy downs of the northern seacoast of France, on the craggy mountains of the Rhine, where they have been made by man's hands.'[3]

In the Weald of Kent and Sussex too, he saw no one in the fields:

> 'I could walk for twenty miles without crossing anything but heath or woodlands, rented as pheasant-shooting grounds to "London gentlemen", as the labourers said. "Ungrateful soil" was my first thought; but then I would occasionally come to a farm at the crossing of two roads and see the same soil bearing a rich crop; and my next thought was "tel seigneur, telle terre", as the French peasants say.'[4]

Kropotkin argued for a peopled landscape and his book *Fields, Factories and Workshops* is not only an exploration of the economic consequences of the humanization of work, but an anticipation of changes made possible by technologies which did not exist when he wrote. For he was writing at a time when Britain was still regarded as 'the workshop of the world', and when it was assumed by economists of both right and left that huge centralized factories were the industrial norm for the future. But Kropotkin argued that there is an inevitable trend for industry to disperse throughout the world, that the scramble for overseas markets is consequently futile, and that small-scale production for a local market is the pattern of future industry.

He concluded that intensive small-scale farming could meet the basic food needs of a country like Britain and that the dispersal of industry in combination with agriculture is rational and desirable and would provide a reduction of working hours and greater individual fulfilment. Education should equip every child for a working life that combined brain work and manual work. Kropotkin was endlessly optimistic, and prophecies seldom fulfil the prophets' anticipations. Certainly industry was globally dispersed, but for a global rather than a local market. Certainly Britain could be agriculturally self-sufficient, but through the opposite of the labour-intensive bio-dynamic farming he envisaged. On the other hand, as Lewis Mumford stressed,

> *'Almost half a century in advance of contemporary economic and technical opinion, he had grasped the fact that the flexibility and adaptability of electric communication and electric power . . . had laid the foundations for a more decentralised urban development in small units, responsive to direct human contact, and enjoying both urban and rural advantages . . . Kropotkin understood these implications before the invention of the motor car, the radio, the motion picture – though each of these inventions further confirmed his penetrating diagnosis by equalising advantages between the central metropolis and the once peripheral and utterly dependent small communities. With the small unit as a base, he saw the opportunity for a more responsible and responsive local life, with greater scope for the human agents who were neglected and frustrated by mass organisations.'*[5]

Another observer of the depopulated rural landscape of a century ago was Ebenezer Howard, shorthand-writer and inventor. His book *Tomorrow: a Peaceful Path to Real Reform* was also published a century ago, and has been reprinted continually under the title *Garden Cities of Tomorrow*. Howard was familiar with the appalling problems of the over-crowded Victorian city and put together a combination of proposals for outward movement. A body should be formed to buy rural land at the depressed land values of his day and develop a town surrounded by a green belt, to give the citizens the benefits of both town and country as listed in his famous Three Magnets diagram. The town would belong to its inhabitants; since, as Peter Hall explains,

> *'The citizens would pay a modest rate-rent for their houses or factories or farms, sufficient to repay the interest on the money originally borrowed, to provide a sinking fund to repay the capital, and then – progressively, as the money was paid back – to provide abundant funds for the creation of a local welfare state, all without need for local central taxation, and directly responsible to the local citizens.'*[6]

LAND VALUES

It is important to stress that his intention was to find a solution to the intractable problems of the Victorian city. He was convinced that once the site values of the inner city had been 'demagnetized', since large numbers of people had been convinced that *'they can better their condition in every way by migrating elsewhere,'* the bubble of the monopoly value of inner-city land would burst. Needless to say, the capitalist property-market ensured that this was not to happen. But Howard was attempting to cope with an issue that has been quietly dropped from the political agenda: the recouping for the community rather than for a landowner the 'unearned increment' in site values that is generated simply by the community's existence.

In this connection, Howard declared that he had drawn 'much inspiration' from Henry George's famous book *Progress and Poverty*. The planning historian Dennis Hardy explains that

> *'It was the idea of land values properly belonging to the community which appealed to Howard, although he did not share George's enthusiasm for a centralised State system as the right way to appropriate and re-allocate the benefits. Howard accepted the kernel of the book, but rejected anything that might lead to more centralisation, as opposed to basically communal forms of organisation.'*[7]

The centralized state has been no more successful. The Town and Country Planning Act of 1947 provided for a Central Land Board which nationalized the betterment value of land and imposed development charges. But legislation in the late 1950s abandoned these provisions. In the 1960s a Land Commission was introduced by another Labour government imposing a betterment levy on land, but another Conservative government abolished the Commission in 1971. In the 1970s, the Community Land Act was equally short-lived.

Our failure to develop the social will to tackle the issue of land valuation has, paradoxically, been worsened by the planning system. Planning permission for housing development can multiply the value of farm-land tenfold, while its agricultural value has already been enhanced by the prospect of subsidy, even though that subsidy may be paid as a reward for growing nothing. In the south-east of England 60 per cent of the cost of building a house in 1997 was the price of the land. Similarly, Ray Thomas of the New Towns Study Unit at the Open University, in introducing the most recent edition of Howard's book, comments that:

> '. . . *as far as land in old cities is concerned, the effect of the planning system has been to maintain prices in spite of the exodus of population. Derelict urban land for which no buyer can be found remains as a capital asset for its owners. The land remains an unused eyesore, but when there is any question of acquisition of the land for public purposes, the price is usually in terms of hundreds of thousand pounds per acre. The implementation of Howard's ideas for what would nowadays be called the greening of the city has become exorbitantly expensive to the public purse'*[8]

Another of Howard's famous diagrams, only restored in recent editions of his book, explained his concept of the Social City. Howard was not, as his detractors claim, presenting a suburban ideal. His garden cities were envisaged with much higher residential densities than that of the kind of urban expansion that became known as 'suburban sprawl'. They were conceived as a cluster, separated by a green belt, around a central city providing those facilities that individual towns could not supply, in a poly-nucleated settlement pattern of city regions: a peopled landscape. And although Howard was writing on the eve of the century when the internal combustion engine was to transform the urban environment, his transport priorities precisely fit those we are aspiring to for the 21st century.[9]

Howard's book inspired the two pioneer garden cities that he initiated in Britain, Letchworth and Welwyn, and many such ventures abroad. It led in post-war Britain to the government's New Towns Act of 1946 and to the building of 28 New Towns, admired and emulated in other countries, and criticized, usually for the wrong reasons, at home.[10] In comparison with other forms of development in the post-war decades, especially the disastrous adventure with tower blocks for the city poor, the New Towns had many virtues, were a lucrative investment of public funds and were more economical in the use of land. The choice of government corporations as the engines of development, and the subsequent disposal of public assets in the private market destroyed, as Professor Peter Hall noted,

> *'the essence of Howard's plan, which was to fund the creation of self-governing local welfare states. Top-down planning triumphed over bottom-up; Britain would have the shell of Howard's garden-city vision without the substance.'*[11]

Both Howard and Kropotkin, the prophets of a peopled landscape, were astute in their perceptions of the issues that would pre-occupy us at the end of the 20th century. A note prefixed to the 1919 reprint of *Fields, Factories and Workshops* stressed that *'It pleads for a new economy in the energies used in supplying the needs of human life, since these needs are increasing and the energies are not inexhaustible.'* In the same year, Kropotkin urged that,

> *'. . . after the cruel lesson of the last war, it should be clear to every serious person and above all to every worker, that such wars, and even crueller ones still, are inevitable so long as certain countries consider themselves destined to enrich themselves by the production of finished goods and divide the backward countries up among themselves, so that these countries provide the raw materials while they accumulate wealth themselves on the basis of the labour of others . . . We should not forget that at the moment it is not only the capitalists who exploit the labour of others and who are "imperialists". They are not the only ones who aspire to conquer cheap manpower to obtain raw materials in Europe, Asia, Africa and elsewhere . . .'*[12]

These two observations remain immensely relevant to our approach to today's global economy and our search for alternatives, and nowhere more obviously than in the production and distribution of food, as Tim Lang reminds us in Chapter 8. In Britain five giant supermarket firms control more than two-thirds of the retail food market and roam the world market for producers, always to the detriment of the local food market, whether in Britain or in Africa and Latin America, where export crops may dominate the demand for scarce and precious resources like water.

In an American context the economist Paul Hawken urges a shift from the Free Trade enshrined in current dogma and in treaties like GATT to the concept of Most Sustainable Nation tariffs.[13] Jeffrey Jacob explains the implications of this proposal:

> 'It is possible that the Most Sustainable Nation tariffs could remove the profitability from a Third World agriculture that relies on the application of chemicals banned in North America and wages calculated to do no more than reproduce a subservient labour force. If, however, sustainability requirements in the North were to cripple export agriculture in the underdeveloped South, the beneficiaries would be the masses of rural and urban Third World poor. With the dissolution of plantation-style agriculture, peasants would be free to turn their attention to growing basic grains in order to address the long-standing calorific deficit from which they and the urban poor suffer, rather than producing luxury crops for First World consumers. In addition, without the power and wealth that come from the ownership of cash-crop export operations, Third World elites would no longer have automatic access to the resources of oppression ... Consequently, in under-developed countries whose economies are heavily dependent on export agriculture, the loss of North American and Western European markets could create an opening for democratic movements, movements that in the past have been routinely crushed by the planter class.'[14]

THE GREAT EXODUS

Kropotkin's reflections remind us of dilemmas we have failed to resolve, and Ebenezer Howard too, the 'heroic simpleton' as Bernard Shaw called him when writing his obituary in 1928, was given to astute prophecy. More far-sighted than most social and demographic observers, he remarked in 1904 that

> 'while the age we live in is the age of great closely compacted, overcrowded cities, there are already signs, for those who can read them, of a coming change so great and so momentous that the twentieth century will be known as the period of the great exodus.'[15]

This was good news, because a century ago there was a growing public and official concern about the consequences of urban over-crowding, where any redevelopment at lower densities brought greater pressures of the dispossessed on neighbouring districts, and of rural depopulation. A report to the Council for the Protection of Rural England in 1997 studied the Great Exodus today and found that:

> *'The available statistics certainly indicate that the urban exodus, while long-established in terms of local suburban-isation around older urban cores, is now the dominant feature of population redistribution across Britain as a whole . . . On the other hand, the scale of the urban exodus does fluctuate over time and it is important to recognise that it is by no means a one-way process. Net out-migration from the main conurbations fell to 78,000 in 1982 before rising to 125,000 in 1987 and then falling back sharply to around 65,000 in 1989, since when it has moved back up to around its long-term average of 90,000 a year.'*[16]

It is not surprising to learn from this report that *'Districts with a higher density of people per hectare have a greater tendency to lose their residents to non-metropolitan areas, all other things being equal.'* Earlier in the 20th century, movements of population were still in the opposite direction, and were thought alarming. One report on the exodus from the villages stressed that,

> *'In some parts of the country we find villages from which the majority of the younger able-bodied men have emigrated, and it is generally the most capable and energetic who go. Side by side with emigration, for the last thirty years and more, there has been a huge exodus of labourers into the towns, especially the large towns . . .'*[17]

But of course the 19th-century exodus was composed of the rural poor, while the 20th-century exodus has been composed of the urban affluent. One of the seldom-discussed virtues of the post-war New Town programme was that, with a single exception, the New Towns were the only official mechanism by which city dwellers with low incomes could join the outward movement of population from the cities which, just as Howard forecast, has characterized this century. The exception was the parallel Town Development programme by which an 'exporting' city's local authorities could undertake 'overspill' development in agreement with a cooperating 'importing' town eager for growth.[18] But in rural parishes, there is not merely no place for low-income newcomers, there is no place for the adult children of long-established local families who have been priced out of the housing market and are obliged to rent rooms in the nearest town.

RURAL HOUSING

In the 1970s the historian of the canals and of the railway network, LCT Rolt, wrote a third volume of autobiography in which he described changes in the village where he lived:

> *'Because of mis-application of the well-intentioned Slum Clearance Act by a zealous Medical Officer of Health, most of the old village cottages I knew were condemned on grounds of their low ceilings, or lack of through ventilation. Even with the aid of the available local authority grants, their occupants could not afford alterations which would conform with local regulations. Consequently, such houses have been acquired by those who could afford reconstruction, executives or retired business men. With the result that they have been 'prettified' beyond recognition and embellished with such things as bogus wrought iron work of welded steel strip, carriage lanterns or wooden wheelbarrows filled with flowers. Meanwhile, such old village families as have survived this upheaval live in council houses on the village outskirts from whence they are collected and delivered daily by special coaches which take them to work in the nearby factories.'*[19]

The span of time between the writing and the publication of Rolt's book is a reminder of several aspects of recent history. The first is that those pathetic and neglected cottages were demolished by the thousand in the early post-war decades as unfit for human habitation before they were redefined as precious relics of vernacular architecture. The second is that their inhabitants were thankful to be allocated one of those raw new council houses, with all the modest facilities that had been beyond their reach for years. And the third is that by the 1990s most of those council houses have been sold on instructions from central government and no more have been built. All attempts to provide 'affordable housing' for rent in village England have to surmount the soaring price of land, an impenetrable thicket of legislation and the vehement opposition of the present occupants of those picturesque cottages. (See Chapter 4 by Alison Ravetz.)

There is a curious irony about the fact that in the first 40 years of this century it was possible for poor city dwellers (often only two generations away from the country in their own family history) to buy a patch of the empty fields that every observer deplored a century ago. Scattered around on the coast and in the country there are little patches of makeshift development with grass-track roads leading to bungalows whose origins in First World War army huts or in converted railway coaches can still be discerned behind additions and improvements. Or they are weather-boarded chalets whose asbestos-cement roof-tiles were salmon-pink in the 1920s but have now, through attracting mosses and lichens, become the colour and texture of Cotswold stone. Some of these settlements are famous, like Peacehaven or Jaywick Sands. Others, hidden in the landscape of Kent, Essex and the Thames Valley, are known only to their residents and to the planning authorities, where many hours of professional labour have been devoted to eliminating, controlling or improving them. They are described collectively as the 'plotlands' because when land was 'dirt cheap' in the agricultural depression, it was parcelled up into plots by speculators and sold, often for £5 or less for a plot, to people who wanted to live out their dreams of a place in the country.

The pre-war literature of planning rural conservation was full of righteous anger about the 'bungaloid growth' creeping over the face of the Home Counties, and demanding precisely the kind of control over development that was introduced in post-war planning legislation. The real offence was that low-income families were gaining the freedom to move into a more spacious life that was taken for granted by their betters. And the result was to turn the derelict farmland of ruined barns, dockweed and thistles into an improvized world of make-and-mend, resembling Barrie Trinder's characterization of the pre-industrial rural scene with its bustling activity as *'a landscape of busy-ness.'*[20]

Our Plotland Heritage

Needless to say, by the end of the century, the plotlands themselves have become part of our heritage. At Basildon, one of the few remaining bungalows called 'The Haven' at Dunton Hills has become a plotland museum. At Dungeness in Kent, a plotland site was designated as a Conservation Area to preserve it from redevelopment, as was the site called 'Holt's Field' in Swansea Bay. But when Dennis Hardy and I attempted to collect the history of the plotlands in SE England, we were in time to gather the experiences of the original settlers.[21]

When we met Mrs Sayers of Peacehaven, she had lived there since 1923. Her husband, severely wounded in the First World War, was urged to live in a more bracing, upland climate than that of Tottenham. They sought somewhere to rent in the Surrey Hills and found them far beyond their reach. Through the publicity (on the back of London tram tickets) of the flamboyant speculator who started Peacehaven on the south coast, they bought three plots and obtained title to the land in 1921. They built on it in 1922 and in the following year opened a branch post office and grocery shop, and lived there happily for many decades.

Mr Fred Nichols of Bowers Gifford in Essex was in his seventies. He had a poverty-stricken childhood in East London and a hard and uncertain life as a casual dock worker. His plot, 40 ft wide and 100 ft long, cost him £10 in 1934. First he put up a tent which his family and friends used at week-ends, and he gradually accumulated tools, timber and glass which he brought to the site strapped to his back as he cycled the 25 miles from London. For water he sank a well in the garden. His house was called 'Perseverance'. The view of those plotland pioneers was summed up for us by Mrs Granger from Laindon who told us how *'I feel so sorry for young couples these days, who don't get the kind of chance we had.'* She was right. None of those settlers from the 1920s and 30s would have qualified for a mortgage loan. And our rigid planning laws and building by-laws have ensured that there is no place for them in today's rural England.

What we witness now is a semi-theological debate conducted by the professional employees of various interest groups on the relative proportions of the new housing needs forecast for the early 21st century that should be built on 'brown-field' sites in urban areas and on 'green-field' sites in the country. What is missing is any discussion of which sections of the population the debate is about. Who is to be housed, how and by whom? Do the would-be rural dwellers of the new century have the same demands as those of the double-garage Range-Rover families who move there today? There is a growing number of people, especially among the young, who are concerned with environmental issues, who reject what they see as the socially useless forms of employment the job market offers, but yearn to live on the land. They are interested in alternative approaches to food production, in alternative technology, and building for themselves the most rudimentary of dwellings, in the expectation that their homes will evolve and improve over time. The numbers of these alternative citizens are going to increase in the next century, as environmental crises impinge more and more on people's lives. One such person is Simon Fairlie, who explains how:

> 'When, with friends, I rented a house with a sizeable garden on a country estate, we were thrown out after three years to make way for a golf course. I lived in a van for two years and eventually, with some other people, bought a bare-land smallholding. To accommodate ourselves we pitched tents on our land. In the two years since we moved onto our land, we have been through almost the entire gamut of planning procedure: committee decision, enforcement order, stop notice, Article 4 application, Section 106 agreement, appeal, call in by the Secretary of State and statutory review in the High Court. All this for seven tents!'

The experience obliged him to master the complexities of the planning system and examine how very slight changes could accommodate *'the radical new forms of development that the quest for sustainability demands.'*

A VERY DIFFERENT KIND OF RURAL SOCIETY

The key argument of Fairlie's outstanding book on *Low Impact Development* is that:

'If permission to build or live in the countryside were to be
allocated, not just to those who can afford artificially inflated
land prices, but to anyone who could demonstrate a will-
ingness and an ability to contribute to a thriving local
environment and economy, then a very different kind of rural
society would emerge. Low-impact development is a social
contract, whereby people are given the opportunity to live in
the country in return for providing environmental benefits.
Planners will recognize this as a form of what they call
"planning gain". The mechanisms to strike such a bargain
are for the most part already written into the English planning
system and there is thus no need for any major structural
changes.'[22]

Fairlie is not bitter about the planning system because he also
knows that without it speculative developers would have com-
pleted the destruction of the countryside begun by the farmers
subsidized to destroy woodlands, wetlands, hedges and wildlife.
He knows that most of us demand a more luxurious but eco-
logically friendly environment than the one that suits him, and he
realizes that all living environments are enhanced out of earnings
over time. So he wants to make just a few changes to the planning
machinery so that local authorities can actually foster experiments
in low-impact rural development, 'some of them carried out at the
margins of society, others designed to cater for more conventional people.'

There is, however, a huge need for changes in attitudes, not
only in adopting concepts of fairness and social justice instead of
greed, but also in accepting the desirability of a peopled landscape.
An important ally is the economic historian Joan Thirsk, who edited
the massive Cambridge *Agrarian History of England and Wales*. In a
new book she traces the various phases of alternative agriculture
in our history, from the period after the Black Death onward.

She traces different causes for each of these times of searching
for alternate crops and for our current situation of over-production
resulting from heavily-subsidized environmental destruction.
Thirsk pays particular attention to those turn-of-the-century
reformers like Kropotkin who sought the repopulation of the empty
countryside through the combination of labour-intensive horticulture and small-workshop industry:

> *'Since far-sighted individuals have forecast the impossibility*
> *of restoring full employment now that modern technology is*
> *daily reducing the work required, we plainly await another*
> *Peter Kropotkin to pronounce the same lesson all over again.*
> *The continuing obsessive drive to foster technology and shed*
> *labour at all costs belongs appropriately to the phase of*
> *mainstream agriculture, and not to the alternative phase . . .'*[23]

All too often a concern for the protection of the countryside is a concern for the exclusive enjoyment of it by the mobile affluent classes and a determination to keep out any other aspirants to rural life. Yet the potentiality to retain or revive vital village services: the bus, the school, the shop and the post office, depend upon the re-creation of a peopled landscape.

When Dennis Hardy and I reported the history of the plotlands, we were hesitant in making comparisons between the experience of poor rural settlers in Britain and those of the rural southern hemisphere because, in most cities of the rural South, the 'unofficial' population of the squatter belt is actually greater than the city's official population. We were conscious of the differences between the experiences of a minority in a rich world and the majority in the poor world.

There are, however, important parallels. The architect John Turner, invited in 1956 to help unofficial settlers on the fringes of Lima, Peru, found that, far from being a symptom of social malaise, such settlements were a triumph of mutual aid and self-help, more useful than governmental housing programmes. When he moved from South to North America he found that the ideas he had formulated in Peru were true of the richest nation in the world, and when he returned to England, after 17 years abroad, he found that the housing situation in Britain fitted his formulation.[24]

It is precisely this kind of geographical link that informs Chapters 6 and 7 by George Monbiot and Nicola Baird respectively. The claim for popular access to land in Britain is our local manifestation of a global campaign.

REFERENCES

1 Croall, J (1995) *Preserve or Destroy*, London: Gulbenkian Foundation

2 Godwin, F (1998) 'Dear Tony . . .' *Guardian*, 16 January
3 Kropotkin, P (1899) *Fields, Factories and Workshops*, London: Hutchinson. Modern reprint, London: Allen & Unwin 1974, Freedom Press 1985
4 Ibid
5 Mumford, L (1961) *The City in History*, London: Secker & Warburg
6 Hall, P (1988) *Cities of Tomorrow*, Oxford: Basil Blackwell
7 Hardy, D (1991) *From Garden Cities to New Towns*, London: E & FN Spon
8 Thomas, R (1985) Introduction to Howard's *Garden Cities of Tomorrow*, Builth Wells: Attic Books
9 Potter, S (1976) *Transport and New Towns*, Milton Keynes: Open University New Towns Study Unit
10 Ward, C (1993) *New Town, Home Town: The Lessons of Experience*, London: Gulbenkian Foundation
11 Hall, P (1988), op cit, Note 6
12 Kropotkin, P (1921) Postcript to Russian edition of *Words of a Rebel* (Petrograd & Moscow 1921) trans by Walter, N (1970) in *Freedom Anarchist*, Pamphlet no 5, London: Freedom Press
13 Hawken, P (1993) *The Ecology of Commerce: A Declaration of Sustainability*, New York: Harper Business
14 Jacob, J (1997) *New Pioneers: The Back-to-the-Land Movement and the Search for a Sustainable Future*, Pennsylvania State University Press
15 Howard, E (1904) opening the discussion of a paper by Patrick Geddes at the LSE, reprinted in Mellor, H (ed) (1979) *The Ideal City*, Leicester University Press
16 Champion, A (1997) *Urban Exodus: A report for the Council for the Protection of Rural England*, University of Newcastle, Dept of Geography
17 Land Committee Enquiry (1913) *The Land* vol 1, London: Hodder & Stoughton
18 Potter, S (1984) *The Alternative New Towns: The Record of the Town Development Programme 1952-1984*, Milton Keynes: Open University Social Science Publications
19 Rolt, LCT (1992) *Landscape with Figures*, Stroud: Alan Sutton
20 Trinder, B (1982) *The Making of the Industrial Landscape*, London: JM Dent
21 Hardy, D and Ward, C (1984) *Arcadia for All: The Legacy of a Makeshift Landscape*, London: Mansell

22 Fairlie, S (1996) *Low Impact Development: Planning and People in a Sustainable Countryside*, Oxford: Jon Carpenter
23 Thirsk, J (1997) *Alternative Agriculture: A History from the Black Death to the Present Day*, Oxford University Press
24 Turner, J (1976) *Housing by People: Towards Autonomy in Building Environments*, London: Marion Boyars

6   THE LAND IS OURS

George Monbiot

In October 1997, a bunch of people in Darth Vader costumes dragged me out of the splintered wood and rubble of London's only sustainable village. Even as we were being removed, the earthmovers were moving in. They destroyed the wooden houses and the gardens we'd made, and returned the site to the dereliction we'd discovered when we first arrived. Sitting on the pavement in Wandsworth nursing a bruised head, this seemed to me a rather odd place for someone with a special interest in rainforest ecology to end up.

Ten years ago, as a rather naive natural historian, I went to work in the far east of Indonesia, in the annexed province of Irian Jaya. Until just a few years before, the forests there, and the tree kangaroos, birds of paradise and birdwing butterflies, had been more or less left alone. But now the forests were being pushed back fast, and I wanted to find out why. The answers weren't slow in coming.

The government was trying to integrate Irian Jaya into the rest of the nation. To this end, it was flying in tens of thousands of Javanese people, establishing settlements for them and giving them the lands of the native Papuan people. The Papuans were being moved into prefabricated model villages and used as labour for logging and planting oil palms. The forests they had used to supply all their needs – food, fuel, shelter and medicine – were seen by the government as sources of single commodities: timber, for example, or land for planting oil palms. This is very similar to the situation in the Solomon Islands described by Nicola Baird in Chapter 7. Control of the forests had been taken over by bureaucrats and army officers who lived far away and were not likely to suffer the consequences of their disappearance.

I became interested in the issue of who was pulling the levers of rainforest destruction and, with that in mind, I moved to Brazil when my work in Indonesia had finished. At the time, in 1989, the received wisdom was that the Amazon forests were disappearing because the colonists moving into them believed they could enrich themselves there. Ignorant of rainforest ecology, they were, we were told, convinced that moving to the Amazon and farming or 'mining' the forests was a better economic option than staying at home.

My findings were rather different. First I found that a rapacious trade in mahogany, driven by consumer demand in Britain and the US, was laying down the infrastructure and providing much of the economic incentive for further exploitation. Then I found that many of the people, moving down the roads being opened by the mahogany cutters, had not so much jumped as been pushed. I went back to the places from where they were coming, and found that, backed by armed police and hired gunmen, the big land-owners were expanding their properties by tearing down the peasant villages, killing anyone who resisted, and seizing the land the peasants held in common. Many of those who moved into the Amazon left their home states because they had no choice. Destruction took place at both ends: where they came from, as absentee landlords destroyed all the different resources they had relied on, and replaced them with just one resource – grazing for cattle, and where they arrived, as the peasants found themselves with little choice but to do to the Amazon's indigenous people what the landlords had done to them.

In East Africa, I came across a rather similar situation. Through both government policy and massive institutional fraud, the land held in common by pastoral peoples such as the Masai and Samburu was being divided up and moved swiftly into the hands of businessmen. The woods, scrub, grasslands and flowering sward of the savannah were being ripped up to produce wheat and the remaining herders were concentrating in the hills too steep to plough, all leading to soil compaction, flooding and drought. The situation was exacerbated by East Africa's conservation policies, which excluded herding people from many of their best lands, ostensibly to protect the game, but in truth to avoid offending tourists. The herders were both set against nature conservation and forced to overuse their remaining resources, while both tourists and corrupt state bureaucracies inflicted, in some cases, far greater damage on this protected land than its inhabitants had done.

Painfully slowly, the penny began to drop. All over the tropics, I had seen environmental destruction following land alienation.

When traditional landholders are dispossessed and either private businesses, large proprietors or state bureaucracies take over, habitats are destroyed. I came to see that rural communities are often constrained to look after their land well, as it is the only thing they have, and they need to protect a diversity of resources in order to meet their diverse needs. When their commons are privatized, they pass into the hands of people whose priority is to make money, and the most efficient way of doing that is to select the most profitable product and concentrate on producing it. I saw that without security of tenure and autonomy of decision-making, people have no chance of defending the environment they depend on for their livelihoods. What Brazil needed was land reform; what Kenya and Indonesia needed was the recognition and protection of traditional land rights. By themselves, these policies wouldn't guarantee environmental protection, but without them you could guarantee environmental destruction.

MEANWHILE, BACK IN THE UK

All this, as well as the appalling social consequences of land alienation, shouldn't be very hard to see, and liberal-minded people in the North have for a long time supported calls for land reform in the South. But, like nearly everyone else, throughout these travels I remained obtuse about the relevance that these ideas might have for northern countries. In Britain, had anyone asked me, I would have said that land alienation was a done deal, and what people had to concentrate on was urging the government to keep its promises and enforce environmental standards. That was until Twyford Down.

At first, I didn't really understand what was going on, or how it related to me. It took a lot of persuasion by some insistent friends to get me down there. But when I arrived, it blew me away. I began to see that this was far more than just a struggle over transport policy. Building the road through Twyford Down was not just bad transport decision-making, but also bad land-use decision-making. It was only possible because of a suspension of democratic account-ability so profound that the decision to build the road was taken before the public enquiry began. What the protesters were fighting was exactly the same sort of remote decision-making, by people who didn't have to suffer the consequences, that I had seen in Indonesia, Kenya and Brazil.

What had puzzled me was that, in Britain, land passed into the hands of a minority of owners and decision-makers centuries ago. The enclosures and the clearances were the culmination of 1000 years of land alienation, but they were as traumatic as those confronting the peasants of north-eastern Brazil today. In England, tens of thousands were forced into vagrancy and destitution. In Scotland, people were packed onto ships at the point of a gun and transported across the ocean to the Americas in conditions worse than those of the slave ships. Others crowded into the cities.

It is so long since we had a grip on land use that these struggles, scarcely recorded in mainstream history books, have passed out of popular consciousness. What happens to the land – the transactions and changes it suffers – is no longer our concern. It's a matter for the minority of people who control it.

Yet it is for the very reason that these changes took place so long ago that they are so important. Their significance has seeped into every corner of our lives. The issue has been invisible, not because it is so small, but because it is so big. We simply can't step far enough back to see it.

Let's look at it, to begin with, purely from the environmental point of view. Environmental quality is a function of development. In the world's wilderness areas it depends on the absence of development. In managed landscapes like Britain's, it depends on the balance of built and non-built development, and the quality and character of both categories. The quality and character rest in turn on who is making the development decisions.

If a decision arises from an informed consensus of the views of local people and anyone else the development might affect, then you are likely to see people's vested interest in the quality of their surroundings, and hence the quality of their lives, reflected in that decision. If, on the other hand, a decision emerges from an impenetrable cabal of landowners, developers and government officials, accountable to no one but shareholders and the head of department, who don't have to suffer the adverse consequences of the development they choose, it is likely to have a far more negative impact on the quality of people's surroundings.

LAND AS A COMMODITY

There is no shortage of explanations for the near-collapse of the Hong Kong stock market in 1997, which precipated such chaos in London. The Hong Kong dollar was overvalued, interest rates were too high and Thailand's baht crisis destabilized the market. Over 40 per cent of the Hong Kong stock market was invested in property speculation. Hong Kong, as we know, has very little land and a great deal of money. The result was a fiercely speculative market in the city's most fundamental resource. Property prices rose to utterly unsustainable levels, and their inevitable collapse brought the rest of the market crashing down.

Britain looks nothing like Hong Kong. We have over 200 times as much land, most of which, happily, has not yet been covered in concrete (though the extraordinary fact that Hong Kong has twice as many farming people per head of population as we do testifies to our astonishing agricultural practices). According to the Stock Exchange, only two per cent of our total share value is invested directly in the property market. We should, it seems, thank Providence that we live on a large island, not a small one.

Yet Britain is also showing symptoms of the epidemic that has felled Hong Kong. Our own current crisis has been preceded by several years of booming property prices. In some cities, land values are shooting up towards the Hong Kong level, partly, and ironically, because Hong Kong speculators have been buying up many of our prime sites. According to London Residential Research, an astonishing 50 per cent of the new homes sold in central and inner London in the first half of 1998 went to buyers in the Far East. Land in parts of central London now costs more than £3 million an acre: even in the provinces, urban land can fetch £2 million.

So why, in this very different and largely rural nation, have land prices mimicked those of Hong Kong, exposing us, like the Hong Kong people, to financial instability? The answer is simple: we too have an absolute shortage of development land, the result not of geography but of statute. Development zoning means that just 15 per cent of the land in Britain is available for construction.

Few people would dispute that this is a good thing – indeed, it is the principal thing that prevents the concreting of the countryside. The problem arises from the fact that this artificial market is allowed to function as if it were a free one. The results are plain for everyone to see. Even people with steady jobs are discovering that affordable accomodation is difficult to obtain in many towns, either to buy or to rent. Rents are so high because house prices are so high. House prices are so high not because bricks and mortar are expensive, but because the value of the land on which they sit has boomed.

Taxpayers pay high prices for housing benefit and social housing costs whose real beneficiaries are sickle-finned speculators. Developers are forced to build only the most lucrative constructions in cities, rather than the affordable homes we so desperately need. At the same time, they are lobbying the government to let them dump houses all over the countryside, where land prices are still low.

It wouldn't be hard to sort all this out. Simple planning policy guidance, listing basic social needs, then insisting that they are met before luxury developments can be approved, would slowly deflate the speculative price of urban land. It would release a huge amount of government spending: more than enough to help homeowners getting into trouble as a result of the adjustment. Society would reap a correction dividend worth billions.

The alternative is to carry on as we are, condemned to a perpetual cycle of speculative overvaluation, social exclusion, environmental destruction and market exposure, followed by violent correction, negative equity and social instability. Our economy, as we are now discovering so painfully, is as unsafe as houses. There are, of course, other ways of doing things.

For example, the land we occupied in London was scheduled for the ninth major superstore within one-and-a-half miles. Local people were adamantly opposed to it, as it would destroy small shops, increase the traffic burden and make their part of the world more like every other part of the world. They wanted the land, which had been left derelict for seven years, to be used instead for what the borough desperately needed: green spaces for their children to play in, community projects to replace the ones that Wandsworth Borough Council had destroyed, and affordable housing. The landowners' proposal was rejected by the council, but that, unfortunately, was not the end of it. Developers in this country have the most extraordinary legal powers to subvert the democratic process and impose their projects even on the most reluctant population.

If ordinary people don't like a local authority's decision to approve a development, there's nothing whatsoever that they can do about it. If a developer doesn't like the council's decision to reject his proposed development, he can appeal to the Secretary of State for the Environment. The developer knows that an appeal will cost the council hundreds of thousands to contest. Time and again developers use the threat of appeal as a stick to wave over the council's head, and as often or not the blackmail works.

If the council has enough money to fight an appeal, however, and if at appeal the Secretary of State rejects the developer's plans, all the developer need do is to submit an almost identical planning application, and the whole process starts again. This can go on until both the money and the will-power of the council and local people are exhausted and he gets what he wants.

If the blackmail and extortion still don't work, however, the developer has yet another weapon in his armoury. Planners call it 'offsite planning gain'. Most people would recognize it as bribery. Developers can offer as much money as they like to a local authority, to persuade it to accept their plans. You don't like my high-rise multiplex hypermarket ziggurat? Here's a million pounds, what do you think of it now?

The results of this democratic deficit are visible all over our cities. Where we need affordable, inclusive housing, we get luxury, exclusive estates; where we need open spaces we get more and more empty office blocks; where we need local trade we get superstores (and I can confidently predict that in ten years time there will be as much surplus superstore space as there is surplus office space today). These developments characteristically generate huge amounts of traffic. Affordable housing is pushed out into the countryside. Communities lose the resources which hold them together.

RURAL RELATIONS

But if this suspension of accountability is onerous in the towns, it is perhaps even more poignant in the countryside. There the message, with a few exceptions, is clear: it's my land, and I can do what I want with it.

Over the centuries, the concept of property has changed dramatically. Property was a matter of possessing rights in land or its resources, and there were few areas of land in which rights of some kind were not shared. Today it is the land itself which is called property, and the words for the rights we possessed have all but disappeared. 'Estovers' (the right to collect firewood), 'pannage' (the right to put your pigs out in the woods), 'turbary' (the right to cut turf), and 'pescary' (the commoners' right to catch fish) have passed out of our vocabulary; now, on much of the land in Britain, people no longer even have the right of access. The landowners' rights are almost absolute, ours are effectively non-existent.

This means the landowners can get away with some terrible things. Every year throughout the 1990s, country landowners have overseen the loss of 18,000 kilometres of hedgerow. Since the war, they have destroyed nearly 50 per cent of our ancient woodlands, and this century they have ploughed over 70 per cent of our downlands. Heaths, wetlands, watermeadows and ponds have also been hit badly.

Most distressingly, across huge areas they have erased the historical record. The dense peppering of longbarrows, tumuli, dykes and hillforts, in what are now the arable lands of southern England, has all but disappeared since the war. In response to landowners' lobbying, the government continues to grant special permission – the Class Consents – to plough out even scheduled ancient monuments. Features that persisted for thousands of years, that place us in our land, are destroyed in a matter of moments for the sake of crops that are not urgently needed. Our sense of belonging, our sense of continuity, our sense of place, are erased.

It doesn't matter how well loved these places were. Even if people had for centuries walked, played, made love in the watermeadows, if those meadows are not a Site of Special Scientific Interest (SSSI), the landowner can simply move in without consulting anyone, and plough them out, destroying everything local people valued. Even where they are SSSI, this seems in practice to make little difference, as such sites are often being eroded and destroyed, in some cases with the help of the taxpayer.

Agriculture and forestry are perversely not classed as development, and are therefore exempt from public control of any form. Even the erection of farm buildings requires no more than a 'nod and a wink' from the local authority. By contrast, if people such as gypsies, travellers and low-impact settlers, people from somewhat less elevated classes than those to which many country landowners belong, try to get a foothold in the countryside, they find they haven't a hope. It doesn't matter how discreet their homes are, it doesn't matter whether, like Tinkers' Bubble, they actually enhance environmental quality, rather than destroying it, they are told the countryside is not for them. You can 'throw up' a barn for 1000 pigs with very little trouble, but try living in a hole in the ground in the middle of the woods, and you'll find all the hounds of hell unleashed upon you.

What we're getting in the countryside is not just a biological monoculture, but a social monoculture as well. Just as in Kenya, only one product is being optimized, and that is profit. The costs to the wider community count for nothing. This accounts for what you see every time you travel through the countryside: mile upon mile of agricultural land empty of human beings, as Colin Ward graphically describes in Chapter 5. It's hardly surprising. Britain now has fewer people employed in farming than any other Western nation. In the city state of Hong Kong, twice the percentage of the population works in agriculture as in the green garden of Britain. Yet we continue to shed farm labour at the rate of 10,000 a year.

Such trends are aggravated by our physical exclusion from the land. People fought so hard for Twyford Down because they had a stake in it; they had a right to walk over it and saw it as their own. When excluded from the land we have less interest in its protection, it is someone else's business, not ours, so, with a few exceptions, we let the landowner get on with it.

The exclusive use of land is perhaps the most manifest of class barriers. We are, quite literally, pushed to the margins of society. If we enter the countryside we must sneak round it like fugitives, outlaws in the nation in which we all once had a stake. It is, in truth, not we who are the trespassers but the landlords. They are trespassing against our right to enjoy the gifts that Nature bequeathed to all of us.

So what are we going to do about it? Well, it's time that we began to see that an analysis of Britain as a Western liberal democracy is no longer relevant. What I have been describing are developing-world politics and economics. We need developing-world tactics to respond to them. And this is what the direct activists, whom I first came across on Twyford Down, saw before anyone else in the country. They saw that we had to take our lead not from our own recent traditions of letter writing and banner waving, but from the anti-apartheid movement in South Africa and the Brazilian land reform campaigns. Direct action is not the whole answer, nor is it an end in itself; but it is an unparalleled means of drawing attention to issues which have languished in obscurity to the cost of us all.

We need:

1 Land for homes: low-cost and self-built housing in cities, places for travellers and low-impact settlers in the countryside.
2 Land for livelihoods: subsidies and planning to support small-scale, high employment, low-consumption farming.
3 Land for living: the protection and reclamation of common spaces, reform of the planning and public enquiry processes, mandatory land registration and a right to roam.

The land, in other words, must start to serve us, rather than simply those who control it. Development must become the tool of those who need development most – the homeless and the dispossessed – rather than benefiting only the developers. For the land we tread is not theirs, it is ours. It is the duty of all responsible people to take it back.

7   Poverty Power: Community Empowerment in Developing Countries

Nicola Baird

Changing the World

At first journalism seemed easy. You asked interesting people intrusive questions, you found out the truth, you got a byline and a pay cheque. Admittedly, working on one of IPC's weekly news magazines didn't change the world, but it kept me in expensive shoes and out on the town most nights. When I wasn't rushing from the office to a party I realized I was wasting my life. So, in 1990 I took up a job as a journalist-trainer for a non-government organisation (NGO) in the Solomon Islands' dusty capital, Honiara. It was arranged by Voluntary Service Overseas (VSO) whose UK-based staff did their best to prepare volunteers for a two-year stint in a very different culture, as much by pep talks on development and racism, as by providing language training. Despite VSO's preparation efforts, it was still a shock to find myself in the South Pacific away from the culture of 'yuppie' greed which had so dominated my London working life. The main issues were about sustainable use of the country's fish stocks, damage to the rainforest by loggers and what was appropriate education for people in a developing nation.

Not surprisingly the experience changed most of my pre-conceptions. After two years producing a magazine for people in a society where literacy hovered at a shocking 20 per cent, written words had stopped seeming so important – action was all. I returned to the UK, to a bank account in tatters, but suddenly with less need to consume. Of course I couldn't grow my own food in a top-floor flat, but I could make my own entertainment, search for organic foods, shop locally and make a point of getting involved in my own community's environmental initiatives.

It took some time to realize I was enjoying the low life, but even at times when I felt positively deprived, compared to the rich and famous of haunting magazines and gossip columns, the memory of the energy and positive changes I'd seen amongst villagers, assisted by the teachings of my bosses Abraham Baeanisia and John Roughan at Solomon Islands Development Trust (SIDT), made sense. They showed me that to engineer change you need to be willing to do it yourself, in a collaborative way.

This chapter is as much about their inspirational ways of helping villagers make difficult decisions about development, as it is charting ways that people, like you or me, can make a difference to the sustainability of the world's environment – especially its forests – using examples from the Solomons as well as Mexico, Zambia and Sweden.

Viewpoints

'What sort of person are you?' asked the grey-haired man addressing his staff as part of the SIDT tenth anniversary celebrations.

> *'Suppose you are standing on a hill, looking out to sea, and you see someone fishing on the reef. Do you think: "What a beautiful day! I wish that was me. Wouldn't it be good to have time for an afternoon messing about in a boat and then home for barbequed fish supper"? Or are you the second sort, someone who sees a bit more? Would you say: "What sort of idiot would go fishing today? The sea looks rough now the wind's picked up and that canoe will be in trouble if someone doesn't help?" Or would you do more than assess the danger? Would you have the initiative to run to the seashore to see what you could do to help save the man?'*

I realized I was in the first category, oblivious to people's problems. All I did was write down their complaints and injustices and then look for another, better issue to write about. I stopped taking notes and looked around – even though the audience, of more than 100 of SIDT workers, had heard the story before, Baeanisia's personal challenge had a surprising effect. There was a sudden hush. All that could be heard was the slap, slap, slap of the college hall's ceiling fans creakily turning. Then a mother snapped a muslin at a mosquito trying to settle on the toddler who'd fallen asleep at her feet, exhausted by the heavy afternoon humidity. The sound triggered a renewed buzz around the room – coconut-biscuit packets started to be rustled again and the betel-nut chewers spat out their lime-leaf goo, with relief, making rusty marks on the cement floor. Working for SIDT they already knew how they helped both villagers and their country's environment by sharing information about the consequences of the developments, such as logging and mining, which people from the city, or overseas, kept claiming would make everyone rich.

Back in 1981, when SIDT started, it had been very different. The organization had been set up by a one-time Catholic priest, John Roughan, who has lived in the Pacific for the past 40 years. At first he did all the jobs: cleaner, typist, driver, publisher, accountant, mobile team director and technical adviser.[1] But once Baeanisia was persuaded to join, as joint director, the organization never looked back in its mission to share information with the country's 350,000 population, most of whom lived in isolated rural villages relying heavily on the Solomon Islands' natural resources to feed their families. These days SIDT has more than 150 staff and is run entirely by the islanders.

Village Empowerment

The Solomon Islands is a double chain of islands about three hours flight north-east of Australia. It is little-visited by tourists, though remembered by many as the stage for some of the most bloody battles between Japan and America during the final years of World War Two. Though the rusted hulks of ships and planes still litter the country and coast, it would still be hard to find a more beautiful country. There are thickly-forested mountains, palm-fringed beaches, flocks of wild parrots and island-peppered lagoons.

For many years the Solomons was a British colony until handed independence, in an ungainly rush, back in 1978. But 20 years of self-rule have left the country in a sad state. There is peace, but the economy, despite bleeding its natural resources of tuna fish and logs in the most unsustainable manner – and usually by overseas companies – is a wreck. In December 1997 the new, but still cash-struck government, perpetually worrying about how to meet civil-service wages and growing import bills for rice, kerosene and machinery, decided its only option was to devalue the Solomon dollar by 20 per cent.

Until recently the cash economy was an aberration for most of the population, so it mattered little that few paid jobs were on offer. Even now 90 per cent of the population live in small, isolated rural villages where they rely on home-grown food from vegetable gardens cut into the rainforest, making use of barter, or the good-nature of cash-earning family members, for things they cannot grow or catch.

In a country with more than 80 languages, the first task was to train villagers to be able to tour their local region and provide information about development issues or running workshops. *'The thrust is sharing information,'* says Baeanisia. *'This gives people access to facts so that they can make informed judgements about how their local economic resources – fish, timber, cocoa and vegetable oil – tie in with the international economy.'* This is no easy task.

> *'Outsiders do not understand Melanesian economics. In Solomon Islands people lived as their ancestors did until the Second World War. There was no cash economy. In a sub-sistence economy once the food crops are eaten you need to grow another food crop – so today people think once your project is finished you just apply for more money and start a new project.'*[2]

Helping to provide villagers with both an understanding of economics, at the same time as assisting them if they object to a particular development scheme, such as logging, has not been popular. Even today SIDT is still accused of being anti-development, but Roughan isn't worried: *'It's a back-handed compliment. It shows SIDT is recognised as dealing in education and that people know we are not in the business of giving money away.'*

But despite SIDT's work over the years, people in the narrow corridors of government house have dismissed Roughan and Baeanisia as dreamers or troublemakers. Both have had their lives threatened by people who feel business deals have been ruined by SIDT-inspired village resistance. Indeed Baeanisia, who has been dubbed 'the Mandela of the South Pacific', even has bullet holes lining one of the rooms in his house from an aborted attack.

Before Their Time

People like Roughan and Baeanisia, with their persistent visions of a better, alternative way of living, have long been the enemy of those holding the status quo. Yet for those who are willing to put all their energy into improving society, meeting negativity, deafness, or more insidious brakes from authority all too often provides added fuel for realizing those visions.

Not all dreamers are on the grand scale, and some remain anonymous – like the people in the UK who have pioneered practical alternatives to the cash economy such as the local exchange trade system (LETS) described by Jonathan Croall in Chapter 9, or the groups which have set up their own 'veggie-box' schemes to ensure regular supplies of fresh, locally-grown vegetables. These initiatives, small though they may seem, always prefigure a larger ideal.

I have always thought of Colin Ward as someone like Roughan and Baeanisia, a visionary, with his advocacy of living cities and better lives for children found in publications like *The Child in the City*[3] and *Welcome Thinner City*,[4] as well as his stirring calls to help people switch to a more humanized, alternative lifestyle, during the years writing his column for the *New Statesman* magazine.

From this simplistic list it is clear that visionaries rarely have anything in common other than their drive – often an altruistic one – to make things better for the communities in which they live. In general they are also pitching ideas a decade, or more, before the time when they will be accepted as either common sense or inevitable. *'Dreaming is the ultimate democracy,'* said Roughan on a rare visit to London at the start of 1998. *'It's people saying:*

> *Listen, we have ideas too, we're not just going to wait for politicians to mess things up more for us, we can do things for ourselves. We have the ideas and we have the commitment.'*

Roughan is following in Ward's footsteps – though not intentionally – he knows little about him. This is probably no surprise as he has spent so much of his life in the South Pacific, mostly in the Solomon Islands where he has long been a naturalized citizen. Together with Baeanisia, who was born on a tiny lagoon island built by his ancestors, he has empowered local people to make their visions of an easier village existence come to life.

Bright Lights

The Solomon Islands is a young country, literally. Due to a high birth rate, most of the population is under 15 years old. But the future generation is dealt with shoddily on the education front. Even those children who manage successfully in the first years of primary school find they are pushed out of the higher education system because there are simply not enough school places available. The result is inevitable: a growing number of dissatisfied young people, badly educated, unable to find a job but nevertheless drawn to the bright lights of the capital city where they hang around their relation's houses putting additional strain on the few family members who do receive a fortnightly pay cheque.

Worse, many villagers, living lives that their ancestors might still recognize, are unable to imagine how efficient modern machinery can be when it comes to stripping their country's natural resources. Purse-seiners can scoop up vital fish stocks and bulldozers knock over innumerable trees in the densely-forested bush within a matter of hours. And they do. But neither Roughan nor Baeanisia are daunted by the scale of the problem. Through their directorship of SIDT they have helped boost the quality of village life: not by throwing money at the region, but by helping individual households understand the consequences of saying yes to a new development. Advice is also given about ways to prevent the endemic malaria; create fruit and vegetable gardens close to the house; build a less smoky cooking site and construct a homemade toilet.

Money equals development is a commonly-held belief amongst those who have not understood the SIDT message. I will never forget the pay day that I watched my friend Patteson, in his ripped T-shirt, interrupt his favourite card game (*kura*), to hold the hundreds of dirty dollars with which the oil palm plantation workers were gambling. *'With this money we could have development,'* he said with a grin. Then, putting the dollars back on the broken table, the men began to make fresh bets. A night of 'high living' was at stake.

To help villagers understand complex, economic messages SIDT spent the ten years between 1984-1994 concentrating on outreach work. By then more than 5,000 workshops had been run by SIDT's mobile teams of villagers, who are either *wantoks* ('one talk' blood relations) or speak the same language as the participants – making them ideally placed to understand local concerns.

The workshops aren't all hard graft. To enable villagers to visualize the consequences of agreeing to a development, SIDT has a team of actors which performs comic skits about logging, gold mining and fishing as well as health education shows on family planning and foods for a healthy diet. After the SIDT theatre group perform their show, in a lantern-lit clearing, watched by most of the village, education workshops are held enabling villagers to discuss what they have just watched. Is logging a good thing? Who should get the money for the trees? What happens when the logs run out?

The battle by SIDT against logging companies, which cut timber in an unsustainable way for overseas export, has been one of its most successful, thanks both to village education programmes and the ability to offer villagers' imaginative marketing alternatives including honey production, paper-making handicrafts and eco-tourism. There are even experiments with butterfly ranching.

Some results have been spectacular. The SIDT conservation-in-development sponsored project experimenting with handmade paper in three villages, Balai, Nazareth and Baerho, has allowed villagers to earn more than SI$35,000.[5] Two of the villages have pooled their profits to improve village life by buying roofing for the church and communal hall and putting some aside for the future. A project to boost sales of ngali nut, grown locally for centuries, which is delicious to eat and which can also be used as a base for cosmetics, helped villagers in Makira province to question the wisdom of signing over their forested land – and ngali nut trees – to Berjaya, a Malaysian-based logging giant. Faced with resistance from local people, the company eventually ended its operations and shipped the equipment to South America.[6]

'*We couldn't compete with the loggers,*' explained Roughan at an education conference in Manchester. '*But, unlike them we promised nothing. No roads, no medical posts, no schools, no airport strip. Instead we could give practical help and SI$10 for every kilo of shelled ngali nuts.*' The nuts were then shipped to the capital, Honiara, where they were sold. '*It was mostly women who brought the ngali nuts, so it was women who were paid and able to put the money to use in their household,*' he added.

In contrast, money from logging-stumpage fees tends to go to men and is more often than not wasted in a 'boozy' bonanza. As *Observer* journalist Dr John Collee, who has lived in the Solomon Islands, puts it:

'The lifestyle of Solomon Islanders has evolved, like the
rainforest around them, over many generations. Their lifestyle
is what guarantees their physical and mental well-being.
When you destroy the individual's lifestyle you destroy the
individual, which is why, inevitably, the health of these
islanders deteriorates dramatically in areas which have been
logged. Their fishing and gardens are destroyed so we see
malnourished children in the hospital. Their social structure
is destroyed so we see crimes of violence and venereal disease.
Their water supply is destroyed so we see skin infections and
water-borne diseases. Their men become drunkards, their
women turn to prostitution, their children buy cheap sugary
drinks and rot their teeth.'[7]

However, with the recent collapse of the south-east Asian economy,
the next few years may be very different. 'The cash economy is
contracting. In the real world you must have a product to sell, and though
trees and fish were sold, profits were filtered off,' says Roughan.
That's why SIDT is now turning its attention from the basics of
development education towards ways of helping villagers change
their natural wealth into much-needed income – but without
destroying the environment or their communities in the process.
One of the best ways to do that in a country whose landscape
is dominated by rainforest is sustainable timber management by
local people. And there is still time, even though numerous
overseas-based logging companies have paid scant attention to
good management. As an editorial in *Link*, the SIDT magazine,
put it after a clash between local landowners and the government
over logging on Pavuvu island: 'The heart of it all is not about logging
versus not logging. The real story is about how this country should be
run.'[8]

CHANGING AN UNSUSTAINABLE SYSTEM

Forest Stewardship

Elsewhere, as George Monbiot also describes in Chapter 6, the
assault on indigenous habitats continues, with alarming consequences for all in the long term. About two-thirds of the world's

original forest cover has been lost.[9] This has wide-ranging detrimental effects because forest loss leads to environmental and climatic changes as well as biodiversity and aesthetic disasters.[10] Despite this, still more forest looks set to disappear during our lifetime, never mind our children's. Indeed Brazil actually lost more rainforest in 1997 (over 11,000 square miles, about the size of Belgium), than it burnt in 1991–92 and which caused such international outcry in the run-up to the 1992 Earth Summit.

One reason that sustainable management of timber is rare, is because the world's forests are still being ravaged by unscrupulous commercial logging companies who find it cheaper to pay scant attention to sustainability issues. However the Forest Stewardship Council (FSC), an international NGO based in Oaxaca in Mexico, is helping timber producers worldwide not just to manage their resource better, but to ensure that the resource will survive in perpetuity.

FSC, founded in 1995, has established a system of good management with input from timber producers, purchasers, suppliers, environmental groups and indigenous peoples. The result is ten principles and criteria which forest owners anywhere in the world can use to secure FSC approval, which is shown by an eco-label.

In a bid to prevent the system collapsing through a glut of copy-cat labels, FSC's key role is as an accreditation organization. So far it has accredited six companies (two in the US, two in the UK, one in The Netherlands and one in Switzerland) whose business is to inspect forest operations worldwide and decide if they are managed to the principles and criteria of FSC. Already more than 10 million hectares of forest have been certified as 'well managed', including forests in the Solomons, UK, Zimbabwe, Poland and Malaysia.

Although FSC is a collective effort by members from nearly 40 countries to improve management of the world's forests, its driving force on a day-to-day basis is executive director Tim Synnott, who has worked as a forester all over the world. He is backed up by a board with members from Mexico, Malaysia, Indonesia, Canada, the UK and Sweden.

As a result the FSC process is as accessible worldwide for large companies, like the vast plantations of South Africa, as it is for community forest owners, like Solomon Islanders, who only own relatively small amounts of land. It is a system which even works

FSC Principles of Forest Management

1   Compliance with laws and FSC principles
    Forest management shall respect all applicable laws of the country in which they occur, and international treaties and agreements to which the country is a signatory.

2   Tenure and use rights and responsibilities
    These shall be clearly defined, documented and legally established.

3   Indigenous people's rights
    The legal and customary rights of indigenous peoples to own, use and manage their lands, territories and resources shall be recognised and respected.

4   Community relations and workers' rights
    Forest management operations shall maintain or enhance the long-term social and economic well-being of forest workers and local communities.

5   Benefits from the forest
    Forest management operations shall encourage the efficient use of the forest's multiple products and services to ensure economic viability and a wide-range of environmental and social benefits.

6   Environmental impact
    Forest management shall conserve biological diversity and its associated values, water resources, soils, and unique and fragile eco-systems and landscapes, and, by so doing, maintain the ecological functions and integrity of the forest.

7   Management plan
    A management plan shall be written, implemented and kept up-to-date.

8   Monitoring and assessment
    Monitoring shall be conducted to assess the condition of the forest, yields of forest products, chain of custody, management activities and their social and environmental impacts.

9   Maintenance of natural forests
    Primary forests, well-developed secondary forests and sites of major environmental, social or cultural significance shall be conserved. Such areas shall not be replaced by tree plantations or other land uses.

10 Plantations
    These shall be planned and managed in accordance with Principles 1–9 and should complement the management of, reduce pressures on, and promote the restoration and conservation of natural forests.

for traditional reindeer herders, as the Sami people of Scandinavia found, because the FSC approach gives people whose livelihoods stem from the forest an equal negotiating voice with the massive pulp and paper producers of Sweden.

So how does FSC-endorsed timber benefit grassroots organizations of indigenous people? The examples below, from the Solomon Islands, Zambia and Sweden, should provide some answers.

Solomon Islands Portable Sawmills

Not long ago experts said the Solomon Islands' unique forests would be logged out within ten years. Like many of the NGOs working in the Solomons, SIDT was very concerned about the rate of logging. In an editorial in its magazine it pointed out that

> *'the saying "If you look after the forests they look after you" has now been scientifically proved. If you log trees you can put SI$1,000 into the local economy. But by harvesting the trees in a sustainable way, collecting and marketing the fruits, nuts, resins and flowers of the forest, conservationists claim you can make SI$6,000 a year.'*[11]

Although loggers operated in every province, the worst excesses were in the provinces of Western and Choiseul. To beat the loggers at their own business and help to provide people there with an alternative to this unsustainable harvest requires considerable skill and investment. The first local group to do this successfully was the Solomon Western Islands Fair Trade (SWIFT), set up by the United Church, with Sam Patavaqara as director. The group trains villagers how to manage timber on their own lands, organizes training courses, like book-keeping or chainsaw maintenance, and tries to get the best prices for FSC-certified timber by selling to European buyers via a Netherlands timber yard.

The first three village landowners working with SWIFT secured certification to FSC standards by February 1996: two years later this had grown to 36 village groups operating on about 38,000ha of land.[12] *'SWIFT is able to succeed because it is providing people with a really good, and profitable, alternative to one-off logging,'* says SWIFT's forestry certification adviser, Willem Quist.

Despite the country's small size it has a higher take-up of the FSC approach than anywhere else in the world. In late 1997 the Solomons held its first meeting to try and develop a national forestry standard which would meet local conditions as well as the principles and criteria of FSC. The interim contact person is Dannie Kuata from SIDT. Other members include Felix Narasia from SIDT's recently-established eco-forestry unit and Willem Quist from SWIFT.

Zambia's Pit Sawyers

Other countries are learning these lesssons. Zambia is one of the few countries in the world where staples, like soap and matches, are often not affordable for people living in the villages. But a timber and carpentry project, Muzama Crafts, in the north-western province, run by Boniface Mutumbwe, is helping provide villagers from the tribes of Kaonde, Luchazi, Chokwe, Luvale and Lunda with a sustainable income. Producers own about 80 per cent of shares in the company through a trust. The remainder are owned by local district councils.

Mutumbwe has a background in business administration, including a spell at one of Zambia's copper mines. Realizing that villagers were having to sell their timber at low prices locally he looked for ways to provide added value. Converting timber planks into furniture was one method, but he had also heard about the benefits of getting locally-produced forest-honey certified as organic for overseas sales by the Soil Association, the Bristol-based certification body. After making contact with them he heard there was a way of increasing the value of timber by better management to FSC standards.

Currently Muzama Crafts covers one million hectares of miombo-type woodland which is worked by 600 self-employed pit sawyers. Pit-sawing, the traditional method of cutting logs into small-enough pieces to be carried out of the forest, is hard work. Once the tree is cut, a pit has to be dug, but it is a sustainable method of producing hand-cut timber as saws can be easily sharpened in contrast to power chainsaws which are greedy for fuel, oil and spare parts.

Muzama purchases cut timber from the pit-sawing groups and then leaves it to dry. Seasoned timber is then sold to the 400 village-based carpenters, or supplied on credit, who produce doors, chairs, stools, ox carts and a range of furniture which is then bought by Muzama. *'The local market offers low prices and does not distinguish between certified and uncertified timber,'* says Mutumbwe;

> *'we believe that FSC-endorsed certification will enhance the cut timber's economic value and provide environmental protection. Once Muzama starts to sell its products on the export market the increased earning will be passed on to the villagers.'*

Sweden's Reindeer Herders

Wearing his traditional Sami dress (an embroidered overjacket and shirt), Olof Johansson, from the National Union of Sami people, started to speak at the Commonwealth Conference & Events Centre in South Kensington, London. *'I'm a reindeer owner. What's good for my reindeer is good for me and it's good for the Sami people.'*

Like the 3,000 reindeer herders in Sweden, Johansson usually spends the hard winter and spring months in Sweden's forests watching his herd dig through the snow for lichen. Despite this being a centuries-old tradition the Sami people do not own land, even in the forests, and that's been a growing problem for the reindeer owners. Although reindeer do not damage the trees, some forest owners resent their presence. As a result more and more of the Sami people are facing legal threats by forest owners in the southern part of Sweden, one clocking up a legal bill of more than £1 million.

But in January 1998 Sweden became the first country in the world to have a national forest standard endorsed by FSC. Already the country has about 2 million hectares of FSC-endorsed forest – and that's as good news for reindeer owners like Johansson as it is for users of paper and buyers of timber for DIY projects. *'The Sami people were in the process from the beginning. Our voice was as strong as other voices,'* said Johansson, who was involved in much of the negotiations.

You and Me

These 'distant' struggles for self-sufficiency can be aided by choices made closer to home. Not so long ago ethical shopping was more about boycotts than positive choice – and the goods on offer tended to be luxuries like coffee, chocolate and craftwork. However, as a result of the FSC scheme it is now possible to buy timber (as long as it carries the FSC mark), confident that it does not come from a 'trashed' forest.

In Britain consumers can now buy more than 1000 different certified products ranging from stick timber, doors and planters to charcoal, pen cases, bread-boards, kitchen utensils and shelves. As it is still early days, some shoppers may find it necessary to look harder for the FSC-logo on timber, but with the spread of buyers' groups worldwide it is becoming easier to locate such timber in local stores.

Britain's buyers' group, including B&Q, Homebase, Sainsbury's, Boots and Asda, was the first to be established, but they are now in countries like Austria, Belgium and Holland. One has also just been launched in the US with 140 members, including the largest DIY retailer in the US as well as the giant house builder, Habitat for Humanity. The Forest Product Buyers Group's president, David Ford, claims that:

> *'By applying the power of purchasing, business can have a positive, lasting effect on the health and future of the world's forest ecosystems, keeping them economically, environmentally and socially viable.'*

This business confidence is shared by reindeer-herder Johansson: *'When people in Europe, or elsewhere, buy FSC-endorsed products they can be sure that they are not buying products which are destroying Europe's indigenous culture.'*

Doing Things Differently

Determination, vision and a commitment to working collaboratively with target groups are what help make groups as disparate as SIDT and the FSC successful. If you think back to Baeanisia's moralistic tale about being witness to a sinking canoe, it should be clear that there are many groups working to ensure better forest management using all the means at their disposal to achieve the best possible outcome. And at last it seems that sustainable forest management, which benefits both society and the environment, is gaining momentum with the help of both strong-minded individuals and grassroots power.

Grassroots power is, of course, not just stuck in the forest. For example in the UK there are the well-publicized activities of anti-roads protesters and animal rights activists, as well as the initiatives of individuals worldwide to improve their own, and their community's, lives by developing their dreams in their own way – again and again proving that sustainable development is rarely a quick fix put into motion by a dose of industry cash. And there are numerous examples in this book too.

What all these schemes have in common is the belief that the world and its peoples should be treated with respect – and left in a better condition than it was found. As this essay has shown, this doesn't need to be divisive. Instead of divorcing communities from their land, organizations driven by vision, like SIDT or FSC, have found imaginative, appropriate and sustainable ways to benefit local people's lives and livelihoods. All also share an anthropocentric bias, something which many past environmentalists have been deeply suspicious about. And this trend, an unsentimental understanding of the intricate balance necessary between people and the natural world, thereby ensuring the best for both, is one which looks certain to continue gaining ground. Colin Ward would surely approve.

NOTES AND REFERENCES

1   *Link* magazine (1990) Solomon Islands: SIDT, Nov/Dec
2   Baeanisia, A (1991) *Orbit*, UK: VSO, Spring
3   Ward, C (1989) *The Child in the City*
4   Ward, C (1989) *Welcome Thinner City*
5   Approximate exchange rate: SI$5 = £1
6   Annual report (1997) Solomon Islands: SIDT
7   Collee, J (1994) 'Forestry Folly' *Observer*, 6 November
8   *Link* magazine (1995) editorial in special issue no 36, Pavuvu Island,

 9 WWF (1997) Global annual forest report
10 Dudley, N, Jeanrenaud, J-P and Sullivan, F (1995) *Bad Harvest*, London: Earthscan, p 4
11 *Link* magazine (1990) editorial in no 8, Solomon Islands: SIDT, Nov/Dec
12 FSC (1998) *Notes* no 7, Mexico, Feb/Mar

PART V

Dig Where You Stand

8 PLOTS OF RESISTANCE: FOOD CULTURE AND THE BRITISH

Tim Lang

I have never met Colin Ward but have read him for years. When asked if I would like to write a chapter for this book, I accepted instantly. Why? Because I wanted to celebrate his impact on me and because I was amused at my own alacrity. What on earth had got into me? I had just made a vow not to load myself up with new work, but to finish a backlog first. Yet here I was breaking my rule at first challenge!

I first encountered Ward through two sources, both defunct. The first was in the weekly magazine *New Society*, which was merged and then submerged in the *New Statesman and Society*, now the *New Statesman* once more. His columns were an endless delight to me, often on the built environment and people struggling to make an insensible world more sensible. He would pick on some issue of interest and write a general case from it. Often whimsical, always erudite and so sane, I loved his humanity. The second source was more spasmodic. Going round the country in the 1970s, one could always get a view of a district from its radical book shop. There was then a flourishing movement of such bookshops. They were/are cultural centres as much as formal bookshops. (Our editor played a central role in one of the greatest of them in the East End of London.) Even in Leigh, Lancashire, where I visited a lot and lived occasionally, there was such a shop; it lasted nearly 20 years. Often collectives, they were a window on the alternative view of the world, wells of radicalism from which students and local libertarian left culture drew. They were a statement that questioning was alive in this town. Everything then was 'alternative': alternative bookshop, alternative agriculture, alternative philosophy, altern-ative culture, alternative presses and newspapers, and so on.

Ward was definitely a name one would encounter in that world. His was one of those authors' names which greeted you and offered another world-view. His prodigious output reminds us that memory can be right on this. It was not just my imagination that he was everywhere, lurking in the wings wherever non-straight left politics rustled. Whether writing on anarchism or utopianism or allotments, or being referred to in the libertarian world, he was definitely part of the general radical scene, a name I noticed, whose books I occasionally bought or read.

Even in these televisual times, the relationship between reader and author can be intensely personal. In a world which is said to be more individualized, atomized and socially fragmented, the relationship between reader and writer takes on new poignancy. It is one of the great anonymous relationships of the modern world. Living in London as I now do, commuting on the underground, train or bus reminds me of this relationship daily. I notice people, particularly the young, avidly consuming a book, wrapped in the text as they hang onto a strap. Whether slim novel or tome, the intensity is transparent. I see myself in this circumstance, not just in the past, today too.

Only a few years ago, I was walking down a road in Notting Hill with a fellow in my little world of food policy, an influential person not known in the movement for emotion, when all of a sudden he melted and said, *'Oh my god, there's one of my all-time heroes'* and stopped to talk with him. He was a successful journalist and screen writer, who had just had a big series on the TV and who held keen and divergent views on food and animal welfare. My colleague knew the writer well enough to stop to converse with him. Afterwards he told me that this person had influenced him greatly through his fearless reportage. We talked briefly of heroes and heroines in our work. It is often said that we need heroes; maybe, but we certainly all like to have people we admire. Heroes and heroines fall off pedestals. The writer we admire hasn't so far to fall. The reader-writer linkage is a more human, fallible relationship; one can disagree, grind teeth but still admire.

This capacity for us to be influenced by someone we never meet, never know, who may even be dead, is strange. As a young social psychologist, I was immensely affected by the writings of Erich Fromm and all the dissident psychoanalysts and psychologists of the 1930s and 1960s. Even in the late 1960s and early 1970s when I was studying, I knew some of these grand old names were slightly 'loopy', some dangerous; but I could admire their daring to question. In the heyday of Freud's hegemony over psychoanalysis, to question the great man's politics must have been shockingly thrilling. I was aware that, in my own era, a similar frisson was engendered by the 1960s anti-psychiatry and radical psychology movements. My own psychology professor had introduced behavioural shock therapy (I mean electric shock therapy) for homosexuals. No wonder I needed heroes when faced with that reality.

To argue that people's world-views should be understood, not forcibly changed, was indeed revolutionary. I never met many of those great questioners within psychology (most of the 1930s names were dead) but they affected my life immeasurably. They taught me to think. They were the bones on which I chewed, offering their thoughts for us mere readers to gnaw on. No wonder the written word has been deemed so dangerous by dictators and thought-police over the centuries. Good old Gutenberg. He started something with that printing press.

We can have the same relationship with some journalists. Although it is fashionable to decry the endless use of columnists and pundits in the media today, I am not ashamed to admit that I really look forward to reading the views of certain people. We might not agree with them, or not always, but we value their view. I am a *Financial Times* reader – it used to be one of the few sport-free zones, but even it is now weakening. I love to read one of its veteran columnists, Joe Rogaly, on Saturday and one of its younger voices, Philip Stephens, in the week. A friend and I used to phone each other in a fury when reading another columnist – happily now departed – for his idiotically right wing pronouncements on social policy. Whether I agree or disagree, I am a sucker for a well-written column. I have long had the same pleasure from listening to Derek Cooper on BBC Radio 4's Food Programme. I chuckle whenever I hear him.

The point about this relationship is that it is personal. With the exception of the pet hate-figures, one can relax with this writer (or broadcaster). You don't even know them, but here are people who voice what you like to think you would voice if you had the time or whose views you respect even if you don't agree. They make you think, from within a framework that is yours but not yours. They are the alter ego. They speak to you, for you and at you. Ward used to write just such a stunner every week for *New Society*. I have no training in architecture, but he reinforced for me what some architect friends also tried to instil in me, namely that building houses is the human expression of social relations in space. The social world is created, not given. Our built environment, he has always argued, can be created by us when so often it is imposed on us. His writing has always been so optimistic. Look, he says, things can be better. See how this or that group has done it.

His book on allotments is a case in point. Written with David Crouch, *The Allotment: Its Landscape and Culture* was first published in 1988.[1] This is quintessential Ward. The allotment, that hum-drum butt of jokes, the quintessence of a parody of Northern life, is looked at and viewed as a vital expression of human desire to connect with the land and to be self-reliant (in the anarchist tradition of that notion). It is shown to be a nation-wide movement, to have a deep and rich cultural history, and on occasions to be a hot political potato, as when allotments are threatened with being built over by houses or a supermarket, or when they are urgently needed to combat war-time rationing shortages.

IT DOESN'T HAVE TO BE LIKE THIS

Half a million households today have an allotment. This is a remarkable link with land away from the home, since the British were the first nation to be severed from the land in near entirety. The enclosures, industrialization and economic concentration have combined over the last two centuries to create a food culture whose main mass connection with the soil and growing plants is via the supermarket shelf or possibly the garden. But that is a private affair, linked to home ownership, the retreat from the public. What sets the allotment apart is that this is a public enterprise with private responsibilities. This, say Crouch and Ward, is the political flame the allotments keep alive. Quoting Andre Gorz's *Farewell to the Working Class* (1982) they argue that allotments are a tool for self-reliance:

> *'For as long as workers own a set of tools enabling them to produce for their own needs, or a plot of land to grow some vegetables, and keep a few chickens, the fact of proletarianism will be felt to be accidental and reversible.'*

This is the kind of policy world that Ward has always revelled in. The interface of state and individual, public and private responsibility, nation and community creates considerable opportunity for both tension and self-expression. And there is no doubt when one reads Ward's articles or books where his sympathies lie. It is always with the community, the oppressed or the seeker after individual fulfilment within a socially responsible context. Ward, as other chapters in this collection amplify, is a great modern exponent of that political tradition of libertarian anarchism, one which places even-handed stress on the capacity of both state and corporation to disenfranchise the individual. Great delight is derived from the struggle of people to throw off the shackles of company and bureaucracy. His view of human nature is benign; his view of societal organization suggests it is usually malign, but could be divine. He invites us to join him in the political challenge to enlighten civic society.

Reading Crouch and Ward, the allotment is a vignette of wider society. It can be used as a vehicle for 'reading' the British. Whereas the Danes and the Dutch have their garden colonies, with small houses they are allowed to sleep in during the summer, the British allotments, like so much, are filtered by the peculiar class nature of our culture. The exact history of allotment plots may vary from region to region, but broadly they were an early form of the 'social wage'. Food might be dear, wages low, but one could dig and grow for one's family. It was heavily a male responsibility. Hence the jokes in popular culture about the men getting out of the house (female domain) to go to the allotment (male preserve). Allotments are ambiguous, however, in that they were, and once again are, for food. They are an opportunity to wallow in economic inefficiency, to step outside the cash nexus. Food may be grown at a cost in time which if costed economically would be prohibitive. Yet, the process is rewarding in itself.

Communities of common interest are formed in sites such as allotment grounds. People meet on relatively equal terms. The plot size is standard. Only one's labour distinguishes each plot. Experience and labour are rewarded by success over time. The allotment offers one last opportunity to connect with the land rather than just observe when walking or travelling through it. They are all that we, the British, have left after the enclosures took the land from the people in a process that was as varied as it was inexorable. Infamously in Scotland, enclosure was by force. The Highland Clearances still echo down the centuries in Scottish politics.[2] The ownership of vast acreages by small numbers of people rankles many and has an important place in Scottish politics.[3,4] In England, too, land ownership has persisted as an issue[5] but less focused on a demonized few and on ownership per se and more often as an issue of access and planning. The focus is on the right to roam rather than on the right to own.[6] Historically, in England enclosure was conducted partly by force, partly by law, the so-called Parliamentary Enclosures of 1750-1850.

Scotland's enclosures have posthumously gained the historical limelight, deservedly so for their colonizing brutality, but England's deserve scrutiny, too. In their classic two-volume treatise on the English village labourer, JL and B Hammond inform us that before 1774 a big landowner could set in train a legal process of enclosure without even letting his neighbours know that he was asking Parliament for leave to redistribute their property.[7] After 1774, when Standing Orders in Parliament concerning enclosure bills were changed, the process could not happen in such secrecy. It merely carried on openly. The Hammonds use Wardian language: *'But [the new Standing Orders] contained no safeguard at all against robbery of the small proprietors or the commoners.'*[8] Thus was land separated from the more humble homes – 'cottages' – and people, reminding us of the wry ditty by US songwriter Woody Guthrie:

> *'Now as through this world I ramble,*
> *I've seen lots of funny men.*
> *Some will rob you with a six-gun,*
> *and some with a fountain pen.'*

The UK allotment movement was born in reaction to this expropriation. No wonder its interpretation and politics are complex. Some argued that to grow one's own food allowed the employer to award lower wages. Cheap food, cheap wages. Giving Welsh miners a small-holding and encouraging them to work in the fresh air institutionalized their lousy conditions underground, while in part appearing to compensate for it. The allotment from this perspective was a new form of patronage. Against this, others in the tradition of William Cobbett's defence of the cottager (in the old sense of someone inhabiting a cottage with land!), argued that it was an island of self-reliance in a world creepingly dominated by interventions from the state and capital.

This debate about allotments may appear arcane today. With honourable exceptions such as the modern 'This Land is Ours' movement described in Chapter 6 by George Monbiot, the appropriation of the land barely seems a mainstream concern. If the poll-driven Blair government can ignore public opinion on hunting, which in both town and country has an overwhelming majority for banning, and 'listen' instead to 250,000 ostensibly pro-hunting marchers from the Countryside Movement on March 1 1998, this surely indicates the demise of land as an issue in formal British left politics and a return to Labour government backing landowners as it did in the 1930s. Labour is now a rural political party too, runs the argument. True, but the issue is what sort of countryside do we want, what sort of food system?

The vast majority of Britons live in urban settlements, have no aspiration or expectation of land ownership, and have an interest in the countryside fuelled perhaps more by soaps such as BBC Radio 4's *The Archers* or Yorkshire TV's *Emmerdale Farm* than by frequent direct contact. There are more four-wheel-drive cars in my road in London than there are in my mother's deeply rural Northamptonshire village! Therein emerges a political conundrum. The country needs the town more than vice versa. In 1991, the Common Agricultural Policy cost European consumers £24.9 billion.[9] Worse, 80 per cent of this direct support to farmers goes to the largest 20 per cent of farms.[10] The big landowners know that they are heavily subsidized because they fill in the forms that get them the subsidies. No wonder polls suggest extensive popular resentment about subsidies going to rich farmers practising intensive methods; this concern is not confined to the British but is Europe-wide.[11] No wonder the hard-liners argue so vehemently; they have to skate faster as they are on thin ice. Leave the countryside to those who live in it and manage it, they cry. Let the supermarkets feed the people, say the modern managerialists. Leave it to the experts.

EATING OURSELVES TO DEATH

This kind of thinking is superficially attractive but ultimately foolish. BSE was its downfall, costing the taxpayer £1 billion in 1996 alone with £4 billion anticipated as the full bill, let alone the ruin of many farmers.[12] The managerialist perspective will not abandon the field lightly, however, and it does have some arguments in its favour. Managerialism knows the reality of skills; it is hard to grow crops or rear animals humanely and productively. Managerialism accepts the inevitability of divisions of labour; not everyone can feed themselves. But managerialism is foolish in that it denies the patent truth that the land is in trouble precisely because of this managerialist culture. The land may look tidy, but it is being squeezed.[13] Supermarket shelves may groan with food, but the environmental cost is considerable – and still a tenth to a fifth of Britons cannot afford to eat a healthy diet.[14]

After years of being dismissed, the environmentalist critique is now widely accepted, so we will not repeat it here. The evidence of damage is too great. Even agrochemical companies know that there have to be cut-backs on usage. But, counter the managerialists, intensive farming, whether subsidized or not, has brought that nirvana for the poor: cheap food. It is true. Expenditure on food has dropped from a quarter of the average UK household budget in 1950 to a tenth in 1990. So what is the problem? Besides the problem of the new poor for whom food costs are still prohibitively high, there is a new problem in that we, the taxpayers and consumers, are paying for the process.

Behind the astonishing 'efficiencies' of modern food production lies another story. Certain costs, notably health and environmental, are externalized. The price of the 'cheap' food is not cheap. We pay for it as taxpayers or citizens under another budgetary heading. The biggest cost undoubtedly is health. One of the greatest successes of intensive production has been the dramatic increase in production of fats. With changes in lifestyles – more sedentary, less exercise – heart disease is now our biggest cause of premature death. The 1996 edition of the Department of Health's *Burdens of Disease* calculates that heart-disease drugs cost the NHS £500 million a year, bowel cancers cost £1.1billion and diseases of the circulatory system cost 12.1 per cent of the total health and social services budget.[15]

The British Heart Foundation Research Group at Oxford University calculates that the total costs of coronary heart disease are approximately £10 billion per year; this includes NHS costs.[16] When you think that 56 million UK consumers spend about £60–70 billion a year on food, this is a considerable extra cost for supposedly cheap food. Where does this extra cost come from? The big sum is made up of details such as: 66 million lost working days, equivalent to 11 per cent of all days lost due to sickness; £858 million in invalidity benefits; £3 billion for lost production in British industry; a minimum of £1420 million in direct treatment costs to the NHS; of this the bill for drugs alone was £650 million; 23,000 coronary by-pass operations annually, and so on.[17]

Another externalized cost is food poisoning. The costs have been estimated as £1 billion per year in the UK.[18] Mrs Currie's salmonella-in-eggs gaffe may have cost her a ministerial post, but it did the country a great service. Previously, campaigners had been beginning to get the issue addressed.[19] Industry's response was either to blame the consumer for poor handling techniques and sloppiness in the kitchen or to look to hi-tech food irradiation to sterilize food before consumers got it.[20] The rise of food poisoning is complex, partly a triumph of the battery, partly cross-contamination in the food chain, and partly more pathogens in the 'reservoir' – nature fighting back. Consumer behaviour has also changed due to new technologies, shopping patterns and lack of knowledge, but consumers cannot be blamed for lack of education. Home economics in the schoolroom has been abolished under the National Curriculum. Where are people supposed to get educated, if not at school?

The point I am making here is that far from being a complete success story, once we begin to calculate some of the direct and indirect health costs of current food policy, it loses some of its gloss. A similar picture emerges on the environment. On pesticides, for instance, the simplest calculation is the cost of clean-up. Ofwat, the statutory water industries auditing body, calculates that the capital cost of installing activated carbon to reduce residues to permitted levels is £1 billion.[21] The combined capital and running cost of reducing pesticide residues is currently being spread at an annual £100 million. We, as water consumers, will be paying for this but the problem stems from 'efficient' farming.

Another environmental cost is shopping. The rise of the hypermarket is dependent upon a car. Retailers promote the car (and sell petrol). One of the big four supermarkets is on record as saying *'new sites are located where safe and convenient access is obtained by car'* and that *'today, we would not open a store which did not have a large surface level car park.'*[22] Today, if you have no access to a car, you are poor. A sane society would probably reverse that; the carless should be rich. Supermarket distribution systems are totally dependent upon cheap energy. Far from being more convenient, hypermarkets are actually making us take more, not less, shopping trips. The average number of shopping trips increased by 28 per cent between 1978 and 1991.[23] Shoppers also have to go further; the distance rose by 60 per cent in 1978-1991. The mileage of trips to town-centre food-shops is less than half those taken to edge-of-town stores.[24]

The common factor to all this is the food retailers' use of centralized distribution systems. Each firm has its own regional distribution centres (RDCs). All food goes to the RDC and thence to the shops. As a result, the food travels much further. Approximately the same tonnage of food is consumed by the British annually, but over the last decade and a half the distance this tonnage is transported has gone up by a third. This is the food miles issue.[25] Really, when we shop, we ought to get a food-miles bill as well. We do, but it is currently invisible. No one pays for environmental damage except the environment itself, unless the invisible is made visible and someone is made to pay the cost. My argument suggests that the costs of current food systems are unsustainable and that apparently more expensive forms of farming such as organic systems are actually cheaper in the long-run.

Against this backdrop of concerns about modern food systems, what relevance do allotments have, or gardens for that matter? Surely, they are drops in the food ocean? Historically, it could be argued, they may have been important, but today they surely are not. To argue that allotments are autonomous islands in a sea of supermarkets may have romance but lacks economic reality.

THIS FRAGILE TENURE ON EARTH

Look around the world and, almost everywhere, there are expressions of deep unease about the land and its produce. The UK may have its historical peculiarities, and it was the first nation to industrialize and ease its people off the land, but it is not alone. Over the last 30 years, environmentalism has forced public attention onto the fragility of our tenure on earth. Public confidence has also been dented in some modern food-production techniques. To people brought up in the 1930s era of crash, hunger and bust, the promise of those 20th-century wonder technologies – tractors, seeds, fertilizers – seemed infinite. There would be surpluses sufficient to feed all the world's family.

In the middle of the Second World War, John Boyd Orr, that great Scottish food thinker and researcher, later to be first head of the UN's Food and Agriculture Organization (FAO), produced and starred in war-time propaganda documentaries arguing just this.[26] Brimming with indignation at the misuse of land and labour, Boyd Orr argued that farms destroyed by stupid policies in the US and Europe should be harnessed with new technology to feed the world. The vision of his film *World of Plenty* was – and still is – powerful. It is magnificent to see a great scientist arguing the case for equality and social justice. But the vision was technocratic. The new technologies were to be put to socially admirable ends. It was a means/ends argument. To be sure, as this technocratic vision was pursued, yields rose dramatically, but so did pollution and rural depopulation.

Today, as the FAO reminds us, the world does have sufficient food, but it is still inequitably distributed.[27] According to the United Nations Children's Fund (Unicef), one in five persons in the developing world suffers from chronic hunger – 800 million people in Africa, Asia and Latin America. Over two billion people subsist on diets deficient in the vitamins and minerals essential for normal growth and development, and for preventing premature death and such disabilities as blindness and mental retardation.[28] The technocratic vision is there, but the social vision has lacked political muscle.

By the end of this century, public concern about the quality of modern food processes and farming techniques would make Boyd Orr turn in his grave. But the sheer weight of evidence is too great now to be dismissed. Soil erosion is back (supposedly a relic of the Dust Bowl) but this time, world-wide, through de-forestation, salination and poor land use. Climate change threatens immense problems for food systems with direct effects on human health, such as shortage of water, weather-pattern disturbance, rising sea levels reducing useful land, desertification and the spread of diseases to new areas.[29, 30]

At the end of the century, even public policy no longer dismisses the idea that citizens should have access to food plots. United Nations policy for the last 30 years may have had the rhetoric of promoting self-reliance, but today the reality is increasingly one of food dependence. Urban masses do not have full access to the land. They are dependent upon imports – both from the local rural areas and from abroad, particularly after the 1994 General

Agreement on Tariffs and Trade which pressurizes governments to reduce tariffs on imports.[31] Where is self-reliance in a globalizing world? Food security today means reliance upon the market – global markets not local markets. Commodity trade rules.

A New Urban Agriculture

Before dismissing the goal of self-reliance as out-of-date in today's global economy, we should pause. A remarkable tome produced in 1996 for the UN Habitat 2 conference in Istanbul by the United Nations Development Programme (UNDP) argued a convincing case that urban agriculture is already a vital element in food security and should not only be retained but supported to expand.[32] Firstly, it is a fact of life; 800 million people grow food in urban space. There may be little in Manhattan, but in some Asian cities the percentage of occupants with some food-growing capacity rises to 80 per cent. In Russia, whose collective farm system collapsed with the collapse of communism, the dacha system, whereby people in towns have access to plots outside, produces one third of all food consumed. After the Iron Curtain collapsed, some World Bank and other right-wing analysts argued that the dacha system could herald a resurgence of entrepreneurial activity in the Russian food system. In fact, it has been a matter of survival. This may be true, argue the less ideologically-blinkered Western food-managerialists, but it is a temporary phase in the evolution of post-communist capitalism. The future lies in the dependency relationship epitomized by the UK, where about one per cent of the labour force works on the land and about ten per cent work in the food economy as a whole. Distribution is more important than growing food. In a land where food rots on farms due to poor storage techniques and inadequate roads and logistics, there is some logic to this.

But in general, the UNDP report questions the managerialist vision of Western efficiency being translated world-wide. And within Britain, there are hundreds of projects and organizations testifying to its relevance here, too. A marvellous report by Tara Garnett for the National Food Alliance (NFA) and the Sustainable Agriculture, Food and Environment Alliance (SAFE) records the upsurge in projects in the UK which fit the UNDP's perspective.[33] City farms, urban projects, school gardens, collective gardens, allotment associations, prison farms and cooperatives, all testify not just to the existence of small, urban growing schemes but to their renaissance. The allotment is no longer alone.

In the Bronx in New York, one urban garden set up in the 1990s sprouted 36 others within a few years and the Merck Family Fund, a supporter of such initiatives, argues that such 'urban greening' has developed from the 1960s.[34] If in the Bronx in New York urban gardens can sprout, why not in Salford? The Arid Lands Initiative, founded by a TV producer who had seen how high-rise living in the Yemen had been made to work sustainably over centuries, founded an ambitious project with a high-rise housing estate in Salford. The one-acre plot surrounding one block has been transformed by a garden, a pond, seating areas and allotments. Food is being grown in polytunnels on the roof and a community cafe being started. Other estates are now emulating the project.

The NFA/SAFE report documents many such inspiring projects. Many are quietly getting on with matters, unpublicized, unsupported, just groups of people doing what they want to do. Others have been set up to capture the new climate of environmentalism, the search for pure food, and community involvement. Ironically, many of these were born in reaction to the peculiar politics of Thatcherism. The lives of the poor were seriously undermined. The health gap between rich and poor began widening again for the first time since the Second World War. In this context, projects like the Sandwell Food Cooperative in the West Midlands are both imaginative and remarkable. This is a network of food cooperatives supplying *'cheap, fresh fruit and vegetables to hundreds of local residents who could not otherwise afford or have access to them.'*[35] If Thatcherism re-introduced food poverty to Britain, it is heartening that on its coat-tails imaginative developments have followed.

Sandwell and many other anti-food-poverty projects give me immense hope.[36] Like others in the food policy world, I travel up and down the country whenever possible talking to people confronting the dreadful growth of poverty in this rich land. We should all take note of these developments. I discern a really exciting historical moment of experimentation in British politics. Governments may stick to tight fiscal guidelines, but people at the bottom of the social heap are organizing and building up confidence to ask for more.

One movement of which I am especially fond is the new farmers' markets movement, as yet small in the UK, but with a great future. In the late 19th and early 20th centuries, many northern English towns built new covered markets. They were a response to evidence of systematic adulteration of food. Throughout the 19th century, an immense and long-term fight was waged by a small group of campaigners and professionals to stamp out poor-quality food being sold to the public. Food Acts were put on the statute books, new local authority personnel were appointed, all to ensure that food was *of the nature, quality and substance demanded* as the first Food Act of 1875 summarized it. The markets were a significant municipal contribution to the societal response to this wider political problem – dear food, low wages, poor conditions, poor health, adulteration and contamination.[37] These markets were always located in town centres and were well serviced by public transport. Great markets like Leeds, Oldham and Rochdale still stand. Others were run down, or, like Wigan's splendid Victorian affair, shoddily bulldozed despite mass opposition. Half the town signed a petition to keep it, but it was still 'redeveloped'.

It is often said that we live in a market economy. We do not. We inhabit a hypermarket-economy. The dynamics are significantly different. In a market economy, theoretically, many producers or retailers vie for the attention of many consumers. Information feedback allows efficiency to develop. In the hypermarket economy, the distributor holds the key to information. Four companies account for two-thirds of all UK food sales today. They have broken the high street and town centres – or redesigned them – and recreated the service out on a ring road. Hence the rapid rise in the distance we travel to get our food. And now, to add insult to injury, the high street is being recreated under the tin roof of the hypermarket itself. Banks, post offices, confectionery, newsagents, dry cleaners, petrol sales, pharmacies and doctors' surgeries are all attracted to re-locate in the tin cathedral, and bit by bit, an oligarchy tightens its grip. Supermarkets' information on our purchasing, through 'loyalty cards', is immense. The good news is that the British are apparently 'promiscuous' in their shopping habits. The word loyalty has become meaningless. Don't misunderstand me. There is furious competition between the Big Four, but they are a new food baronial class. If you are a small farmer, you do not produce enough to warrant sales to the giants. Hence the importance of the new farmers' markets.

New Rules of Engagement

In the US, farmers' markets began earlier in the 20th century. Dr Harriet Festing of Wye College has lovingly catalogued their impact.[38] More than 20,000 US farmers sell produce through 2400 farmers' markets. There is even one on Wall Street. In the autumn of 1997, Bath City Council, with various green groups, held three monthly markets in which small, local producers brought produce for sale on a Saturday. It was a 'smash hit' and attracted many enquiries from other authorities.[39] The point is simple: that if we actually want a market economy, in which diversity and locality go hand-in-hand, we will have to re-create one. If we want food to come to us, rather than both the food and us travelling further, we will need to create a different set of economic 'rules of engagement'. We will have to build up pressure on politicians to encourage this. Who knows if the farmers' markets movement will take off here? It deserves to, and with supermarkets now approaching saturation and madly having to diversify to keep up their speed on the treadmill, new opportunities abound outside. Supermarkets are vulnerable precisely because they are so powerful.

Part of this vision for the future should surely be a re-think on food education. Here again the NFA/SAFE report on projects is inspiring. A project in Sheffield has been experimenting with healthy eating. In the US, the National Gardening Association has pioneered a 'Grow-Lab' project for schools[40] and the National Science Foundation sponsors more than 50 'Life-Labs'.[41] Both are systems experimenting with teaching urban pupils about how to grow food and to integrate practical with academic skills.

In the far north of Russia, when I was lecturing on a 1996 Summer School for public health officials from all over the former USSR, we visited a remote school near the former Workers' Holiday Camp in the forest below Arkhangelsk, where all children are taught how to till the soil, care for it, plant and husband crops, store and cook them. When the World Health Organization group, of which I was a member, expressed great admiration, the teacher was bemused. *'But what else should one do?'* We informed him that coming soon from the West was a different model, which would have great attraction but could bring a new dependency.

The challenge is to extract the best of both, not the worst, in both East and West. And the good news on our home turf is that teachers in the UK have come to similar conclusions as our Russian guide. There are people like Mark Penfold, a French teacher at Abington High School in Leicestershire, who set up an organic garden in the school. It was so successful that pupils came back in their holidays to maintain it.[42] One has to ask why it should be a French teacher who saw the opportunity to develop a garden, which used food as a vehicle for meeting National Curriculum requirements to study life cycles, but perhaps we should merely applaud rather than wonder.

Such activities are a testament to the capacity of people to see the world, act on it intelligently and to make it better. In a world which is sometimes characterized as inhabited by couch potatoes, it is heartening to observe people actually growing potatoes. People can and do struggle to improve their lives. It is a warming, appropriate and truly Wardian conclusion to draw.

REFERENCES

1 Crouch, D and Ward, C (1988) *The Allotment: Its Landscape and Culture*, London: Faber and Faber
2 Prebble, J (1969) *The Highland Clearances*, Harmondsworth: Penguin
3 Wightman, A (1996) *Who owns Scotland?* Edinburgh: Canongate Books
4 Scottish Office (1998) Land Reform Policy Group: *Identifying the Problems*, Edinburgh: Scottish Office. February
5 Norton-Taylor, R (1982) *Whose Land is it Anyway?* Wellingborough: Turnstone Press
6 Shoard, M (1980) *The Theft of the Countryside*, London: Maurice Temple Smith
7 Hammond, JL and Hammond, B (1948) *The Village Labourer. Volume 1*, London: Guild Books (Longman, Green and Co), p 37
8 Ibid, p 68 ff
9 Ministry of Agriculture, Fisheries and Food (1992) *Agriculture in the UK: 1991*, London: HMSO
10 House of Lords (1992) *Development and Future of the Common Agricultural Policy*, HL Paper 79–1, HMSO

11 See the deep analysis of the Eurobarometer survey in National Consumer Council (1990) *Consumers and the Common Agricultural Policy*, London: HMSO

12 DTZ Pieda Consulting (1998) *The Economic Impact of BSE on the UK economy*, Edinburgh (for HM Government)

13 Harvey, G (1997) *The Killing of the Countryside*, London: Jonathan Cape

14 Leather, S (1996) *The Making of Modern Malnutrition*, London: Caroline Walker Trust

15 NHS Executive (1996) *Burdens of Disease*, London: DoH

16 BHF (1998) *CHD statistics – Economic Costs*, Oxford: British Heart Foundation Research Group

17 1993–94 figures; British Heart Foundation (1996) *Coronary Heart Disease statistics* London: BHF

18 Roberts, J (1995) 'The socio-economic costs of foodborne infection', unpublished paper to Oxford Brookes University conference *Foodborne disease: consequences and prevention*, St Catherine's College Oxford, April

19 London Food Commission (1997) *Food Adulteration and how to beat it*, London: Unwin Hyman

20 Webb, A and Lang, T (1989) *Food Irradiation: the myth and the reality*, Wellingborough: Thorsons

21 Ofwat (1997) *1996-7 Report on the financial performance and capital investment of the water companies in England and Wales*, London: Ofwat, October

22 Quoted in Raven, H and Lang, T (1995) *Off our Trolleys?* London: Institute for Public Policy Research

23 Ibid

24 Whitelegg, J (1994) *Driven to shop*, London: Eco-logica & Sustainable Agriculture, Food and Environmental Alliance

25 Paxton, A (1994) *The Food Miles Report*, London: Sustainable Agriculture, Food and Environment Alliance

26 Boon, T (1997) 'Agreement and disagreement in the making of World of Plenty' in Smith, DF, ed, *Nutrition in Britain: Science, scientists and politics in the twentieth century*, London: Routledge, pp 166–189

27 Alexandratos, N, ed (1995), *World Agriculture: Towards 2010*, An FAO Study, Chichester: John Wiley and Son

28 Unicef (1995) *Food, Health and Care: the UNICEF vision and strategy for a world free from hunger and malnutrition*, New York: United Nations Children's Fund, p 1

29 McMichael, AJ, Haines, A, Slooff, R and Kovats, RS, eds (1996) *Climate Change and Human Health*, Geneva: World Health Organisation, UN Environment Programme, World Meteorological Organization

30 McMichael, AJ and Haines, A (1997) 'Global climate change: the potential effects on health', *British Medical Journal*, 315, pp 805–9

31 Lang, T (1996) 'Food Security: does it conflict with globalization?', *Development*, 1996:4, pp 45–50

32 UNDP (1996) *Urban Agriculture: food, jobs and sustainable cities*. Publication series for Habitat 2 conference, vol 1, New York: UNDP

33 Garnett, T (1996) *Growing Food in Cities*, London: National Food Alliance & Sustainable Agriculture, Food and Environment Alliance

34 Taylor, B (1994) America's urban gardens, *Resurgence*, 176, pp 42–43

35 Garnett, T (1996) op cit, Note 33, Case 13, p 34

36 Leather, S and Lobstein, T (1994) *Food and Low Income: a practical guide for advisors and supporters working with families and young people on low incomes*, London: National Food Alliance

37 Paulus, I (1974) *The Search for Pure Food*, Oxford: Martin Robertson

38 Festing, H (1997) *Farmers' Markets: An American Success story*, Bath: Eco-logic Books

39 Tutt, P and Morris, D (1998) *Bath Farmers' Market – A Case Study*, Bath: Eco-logic Books

40 Grow-Lab (n.d.) *Activities for Growing Minds* and *A Complete Guide to Gardening in the Classroom*, Burlington: Grow-Lab, 180 Flynn Avenue, Burlington, Vermont 05401, US

41 Life-Lab (n.d.) *LifeLab: a growing adventure* (pack), Santa Cruz: Life-Lab Science Program, 1156 High Street, Santa Cruz, CA 95064, US

42 Brown, M (1995) 'School garden', *Henry Doubleday Research Association News*, 141, autumn, pp 24–25

9 Local, Mutual, Voluntary and Simple: The Power of Local Exchange Trading Systems

Jonathan Croall

'To say that people cannot exchange value with one another because there is no money is like saying you cannot build a house because you have no feet and inches' Allan Watts

During the 1990s Local Exchange Trading Systems – popularly known as LETS – have been mushrooming on the margins of society in the UK. Thousands of people, many of them unemployed or on low wages, have plugged into these radical and people-friendly local currency networks. For many, belonging to a LETS has brought real financial, social or psychological benefits; in some cases it has transformed their lives.

So what exactly is the appeal of LETS? What are the real benefits and drawbacks? Is the idea likely to present a real challenge to the mainstream economy? And will it survive into the new millennium? In this essay I examine these and other questions, using material I gathered during recent visits to LETS groups in the UK and Ireland.

SIMPLE BUT SUBVERSIVE

Colin Ward has pinpointed the essential elements of any alternative currency system. In 1995 he wrote:

> *'Ever since Robert Owen or Proudhon, people have been inventing alternatives to cash; and the lesson of the failure of them all is that, to have the slightest chance of being useful, they should be local, mutual, voluntary and, above all, simple.'*[1]

The basic philosophy of LETS is certainly a simple as well as a subversive one: that people don't need money in order to buy and sell goods and services, that they can create their own currency and wealth, and in doing so help themselves, their neighbours, the local economy and the wider community.

The size, style and approach of LETS differ considerably, but all have certain features in common. A system is run by a small core group of people, who create their own currency, compile a directory listing the goods and services members want or can offer, and keep and circulate records of transactions. Members are encouraged to trade, but are asked not to go too deeply into credit or debit. When people start to trade with each other, they may do so on the basis of an agreed rate, price or number of hours. Alternatively the terms may be negotiable between the parties involved in a transaction.

Trading is done through a unit of exchange of the local currency. This may be equal in value to the national currency unit; or be linked to it, but 'floating' in value; or be related in some way to an hour's work. Many groups go for the 'floating' option for ideological reasons, believing that the less their system is linked to the mainstream economy, with its attendant interest rates, inflation, scarcity, and devaluation, the better. Some groups base their rates on a desire to narrow the gap between traditionally highly-paid professional services and lower-paid activities such as cleaning or gardening.

Local currencies have a dazzling variety of names. Many have a monetary flavour, either ancient or modern (talents, groats, pledges). Some groups have opted for a name drawn from their native language (*ddraig*, dragon; *luach*, value; *quine*, woman), while others have used the names of rivers or other local landmarks (solents, tweeds, beacons). A number of currencies reflect an area's industrial history (bobbins, tins, anchors), while others evoke a more romantic or mystic past (reivers, merlins).

The goods and services listed in LETS directories (usually known as 'wants' and 'offers') reflect the nature of the locality and membership. In predominantly middle-class rural areas they are often top-heavy with alternative therapies: acupuncture, counselling, foot massage, movement therapy, reflexology, yoga, stress relief, and so on. Arts and crafts also tend to feature heavily in such groups: punch-needle embroidery, tie-dying, bead-jewellery making, candle making, leatherwork, dried-flower arranging.

Many such schemes list produce – organic vegetables, homemade bread, goat's milk. Others cater for more mundane needs, offering repairs and maintenance, building and construction, gardening, washing and ironing, shopping, dog walking and pet sitting.

Most systems confine activity to their own membership. But as numbers have grown, so the idea of 'inter-trading', or setting up a 'Multi-LETS' with neighbouring LETS, has developed. Inter-trading requires convertibility between local currencies, or the creation of a new one, but is now widespread, especially in rural areas. The scheme involves all the accounts of the individual system being centralized under one 'registry'. Once a person joins a registry, they can open accounts with any system within the Multi-LETS, thereby gaining access to a wider range of goods and services.

THE NEED FOR ALTERNATIVES

The growth of interest in LETS has come at a time when the global market economy is relentlessly tightening its grip on all our lives. Increasingly our communities are dominated by decisions made by multi-national companies, and by the international banks and financiers who control the supply of money. The World Bank reports that as much as 95 per cent of global money circulation is speculative, and less than five per cent related to real commodity trade. Already, hidden interest accounts for between one-third and a half of UK spending.

The pressure on individual enterprise is growing. In the UK the number of small shops has halved in the last thirty years; by the beginning of the new millennium almost half of what we spend our money on will be provided by just 250 companies. Meanwhile just 0.1 per cent of the UK population owns 50 per cent of the sterling wealth.

These trends are having a devastating effect on many of our communities, where money is in short supply; small businesses are collapsing at an alarming rate, and high rates of unemployment have become a permanent feature. It's hardly surprising that this has led in many areas to a breakdown of community values, and an increase in social isolation, especially amongst the poorer sections of society.

Many local initiatives have been launched in an attempt to counter these trends, including community businesses, credit unions, and self-build schemes (see Chapter 4). In some areas these have made a real impact, giving people more control over their lives, and helping to revitalize rundown or fragmented communities. The LETS idea stands firmly in this tradition.

CURRENCIES OLD AND NEW

A LETS is essentially an old idea in new clothing. It does of course have close links with the traditional notion of barter, which has been used as a method of exchanging goods ever since communities have existed. Yet barter has obvious limitations, since it involves a transaction between two parties who may not be able to match each other's needs.

There have been many currency experiments in the last two centuries. One of the most notable was the National Equitable Labour Exchange, set up in 1832 by the radical social reformer and visionary Robert Owen, to help unemployed people meet each other's needs. The exchange printed its own currency in the form of Labour Notes, expressed in terms of hours. While it was briefly successful, its eventual failure was due in part to the fact that it was unable to supply such workers with the commodity they needed most: food.

The idea that the state should have a monopoly on the right to mint coins and print paper-money is a comparatively recent one. Until the Bank Charter Act of 1844 gave it this right, local currencies had been the norm. Often during the Industrial Revolution the coin of the realm ran short, and local banks issued notes for circulation within their area. Some large employers actually paid their workers in their own printed currency or token coinage, which was accepted outside their home town.

Local currencies flourished again in Europe and America during the Depression of the 1930s. One of the most successful was that used in Wörgl in Austria, where it solved the town's tax and employment crisis and changed poverty to prosperity in just one year. About 200 other communities in Austria decided to follow suit until the Central Bank, fearing it would lose control over the money supply, threatened Wörgl council with legal proceedings, and killed off the experiment.

The mutual-aid element of LETS also has historical antecedents in the UK, notably in those working-class communities where people built up their sick clubs, coffin clubs, penny banks and building societies. Such communities were commonplace in the Britain of the 1930s, and helped families to survive in a time of high unemployment and economic depression. In the 1970s there was a revival of interest in mutual aid schemes, varying from Link Opportunity, which initially focused on retired people, to the skill-swapping scheme based at Centerprise, a community bookshop in Hackney. Mutual aid has also been strong in Ireland, based on the *meitheal*, a system of favours done within and between farming communities that is only now dying out.

TAKING ROOT

In the last 15 years LETS has become a global phenomenon. In Australia there are more than 200 groups, while France and Italy each has more than 100. Numbers are growing rapidly in other European countries, as well as in places as far apart culturally and politically as Japan and South America. In the US a bewildering variety of community currency and 'time dollar' schemes has been established.

But there's no doubt that the idea has developed most spectac-ularly in the UK and that, after a slow start, LETS has now taken root. The growth has been startling: in the late 1980s there were no more than half-a-dozen groups, yet by 1997 there were over 400, involving some 35,000 people. About 35 of these were in Scotland, 20 in Wales and three in Northern Ireland. A further 30 were up and running in Ireland.

The basic LETS model for these groups has been the one set up by a community activist in Canada in the early 1980s. Michael Linton lived in the small mining community of Courtenay on Vancouver Island, where unemployment was high after closure of the local mine. He and others tried unsuccessfully to use barter to make a living. He then devised a system which put barter onto a non-profit making, community-wide basis, using a specially created currency known as the 'green dollar'. In 1985 he introduced the idea of LETS to the UK at The Other Economic Summit, a forum for 'new economics' thinkers.

The early LETS groups in the UK and Ireland tended to be set up in small towns or rural areas, within a well-defined and predominantly middle-class community. Many were started by people active in environmental politics, the green movement or the Green Party. But as the idea spread to the larger towns and cities, the social composition of LETS began to broaden, and the proportion of unemployed members to increase. As the recession bit deeper in the early 1990s, groups began to spring up in inner-city areas and on large estates, where unemployment rates were particularly high. While it was often community development workers and other professionals who started the ball rolling in these places, many people on low or no incomes began to participate.

ON THE GROUND

In spring 1997 I visited ten LETS groups in the UK and Ireland, and talked or corresponded with members from about three dozen others, as the basis of my research for *LETS Act Locally*, a book commissioned by the Calouste Gulbenkian Foundation.[2] My aim was to go beyond the slogans, theories and academic questionnaires with which the field was already littered, and talk directly to the people involved. I wanted to find out why LETS was taking off in so many diverse communities and drawing in individuals from all walks of life. I hoped to discover what benefits people felt they had gained from their involvement in a LETS, as well as to identify the problems they encountered. I also wanted to see whether LETS was likely, as some had said, to be only a passing fashion, nothing more than a product of the recent recession.

In my travels I discovered an impressive variety of LETS, large and small, in cities, towns and rural areas alike. Inevitably their achievement varied. A few were vibrant and clearly thriving, a good many were ticking over unobtrusively but steadily, while a few were clearly struggling, or even becalmed. A handful had actually closed down, as the early enthusiasm waned or key people moved on.

One of the most successful was Stroud LETS, set up in 1990. A Gloucestershire town of 15,000 people, Stroud has a long tradition of radical politics and artistic activity. It boasts the UK's first council to be run by the Green Party, and has become a magnet for those attracted to the idea of an alternative lifestyle. The town and its surrounding valleys are bristling with self-employed people, offering everything from tree care to craniosacral therapy, from environmental home audits to desktop publishing.

The LETS, embracing both Stroud itself and its surrounding villages, seems well-grounded in the everyday life of the community. Trading is done with 'strouds', and the group has an office in town manned by a rota of part-time administrators, with a computer system set up with the help of a council grant. After reaching a plateau, membership started to increase again, and by spring 1997 there were 320 active members.

Transactions in Stroud have enabled people to get the services they need even if they don't have the necessary sterling. It has also prompted people to try out or develop skills they don't normally use. So the local doctor mends bicycles, a desktop publisher reads tarot cards, a professional translator does landscape gardening, a retired executive mends toasters in exchange for housework now that his wife is ill. Meanwhile meals at the local wholefood cafe are paid for partly in strouds, which the owner uses to have the premises re-wired. As with other groups, trading makes good use of people's time, energy and talents.

The group's membership is mainly middle-class, and includes accountants and solicitors. Small businesses have come and gone within the system. At one time a firm of solicitors joined, on the basis that belonging brought in custom from people who would not normally use a solicitor. The present membership includes the local Steiner School, which takes 10 per cent of parents' fees in strouds. Two local food traders also belong.

Despite its success, there is a down-side to the growth of Stroud LETS. With new members still joining, it has reached a level where most individuals no longer know most of their fellow traders. Inevitably, people have a weaker sense of ownership of the scheme than they had in the pioneering days.

GETTING A LIFE

The benefits of an involvement in LETS appear to be many and varied. Belonging has allowed people of all kinds of backgrounds to use neglected, undervalued or new skills; given them access to goods and services which they might not normally be able to afford; helped them to improve their personal confidence and self-esteem; and, by combating isolation, widened their social contacts and network of friends.

LETS have perhaps been of most value to unemployed people: on average about a quarter of those involved are in this category. For people living in such circumstances, or those on very low incomes, the chance to trade can open up all kinds of horizons. And since trading is interest-free, they can obtain many essential goods and services without the need for any capital outlay.

Involvement in a group has also helped many people to keep in touch with the labour market, often providing a stepping-stone into paid work, and even in some cases the opportunity to set up their own business. It has helped many to sustain their specialist skills, or to develop new ones. Many LETS groups contain individuals, some of them disabled, who feel their lives have been radically improved as a result of joining.

Another benefit, especially in the larger LETS, is the wealth of learning opportunities available through tuition in various skills or subjects. These can vary from the severely practical to the gently philosophical, and in some places offer a programme as rich as any in an adult education college, where fees have increased substantially in recent years.

Trading in goods through a LETS also has the advantage of forging closer links between the producer and consumer, and enabling people to become more aware of the variety of local products available. Many LETS members prefer this to the more impersonal transactions in the mainstream economy, where most products are bought in supermarkets and superstores from large companies based outside the locality.

Individual testimonies also suggest that LETS have enhanced the spirit and identity of many communities, helping to break down the barriers between existing interest groups and generations. They cut across age and class barriers to embrace old and young people, the prosperous and the poor, the employed and unemployed. When a LETS works it becomes a form of extended family, encouraging mutual support of many kinds.

A LETS can also bring general environmental benefits, since its basis is sustainability. The sharing or loan of goods and equipment is encouraged, so making the repairing and recycling of them more affordable, but also reducing pressure on the earth's finite resources.

People then have less need to buy costly consumer items created from scarce and non-renewable materials. Meanwhile, the more trading that goes on involving local producers and shops, the less need there is to bring in goods from other regions or countries. Such sustainability reduces transport and fuel costs, which in turn eases the pressure on the road system. It also cuts energy costs and levels of pollution in the atmosphere, thereby contributing to the battle against global warming.

PROBLEMS AND PERCEPTIONS

Contrary to the expectations of most outsiders or newcomers, it seems to be rare indeed for a system to be seriously abused by an individual. A LETS depends to a great extent on mutual trust, and examples of members being excluded for malpractice, or of going into massive debit and leaving the area, are surprisingly few and far between.

One widespread problem is people's initial worry about being in 'debt'. It takes a while for newcomers to a LETS to be convinced the system will benefit if they go into debit early on, because by doing so they are stimulating trade. They find it difficult to grasp the principle that the 'debt' is to the community rather than to an individual. Even when they understand that no interest will be incurred, they may still be reluctant to take the first step.

Problems are also caused by people's perceptions of a LETS, and what it can offer. Some groups are seen as middle-class enclaves, and with good reason. Many directories, especially those in small towns and rural areas, conjure up a vision of the membership devoting their entire spare time to massaging and counselling each other. Groups are often seen simply as part of the alternative culture, and therefore somehow not respectable.

People's initial response to LETS often depends on the kind of language used to advertise or promote a group. Unfortunately much of the early publicity was created by people with a special interest in the theory of money, interest and local currencies, who seemed to find it impossible to avoid using jargon. For example, the literature put out by LETS advocates targeting estates in Manchester and Glasgow promoted abstract ideas that proved alienating to residents there.

The notion of inter-trading between systems can sometimes cause divisions within a group. Many people believe the beauty of a LETS is that it is rooted in a particular community, and that any departure from that notion lessens its value. Others feel that if LETS is to develop as an alternative economy, then inter-trading is essential, since it provides access to a wider range of goods and services.

PASTURES NEW

As the network of LETS has grown, so their potential for development in different areas of life is being explored more thoroughly. Innovatory schemes have shown how LETS can be used to enhance some of the most basic aspects of our lives, such as food, health, housing and education. Other developments include the setting-up of credit unions, the appearance of women's LETS groups, plans for an arts LETS, and the growing involvement of voluntary organizations.

As high unemployment persists and local services continue to suffer cutbacks, many councils are starting to see LETS as a valuable element in their economic development, Local Agenda 21 or anti-poverty strategies. A few, operating in some of the most disadvantaged communities in the UK, have even begun to act as catalysts in getting groups off the ground.

By the spring of 1997 it was estimated that 25 per cent of LETS in the UK were receiving help of some kind from their local authority. In many cases the support has been relatively modest: providing groups with equipment, offering them help with publicity and meeting rooms, giving access to internal mail systems, or assisting with the printing of posters and leaflets. In some areas existing or potential LETS groups have been offered modest start-up grants. In a few the council has gone a step further, and actually joined the LETS.

But the response to this kind of help has, understandably, been mixed. Many people believe a LETS should be self-sufficient, or that it should grow organically from the bottom upwards at a natural pace. Others are simply deeply suspicious of, or hostile to, any set-up initiated or supported by their local council.

THE WAY AHEAD

The LETS movement has reached an interesting but critical stage. There is enough experience around for it to have become clear what the main barriers are to further development. If LETS are to grow and thrive into the next century, there are several issues that need to be addressed.

Undoubtedly the most critical one concerns the UK government's attitude to the benefits question. If LETS are to have any real and lasting impact on the poorest and most disadvantaged sections of our society, then people who are unemployed or on low incomes will need to be confident that they can join and trade in a system without there being any danger of their benefits being lost. At present they cannot be so confident, because judgement on these matters is left in the hands of officials in local Department of Social Security offices, and is therefore arbitrary, inconsistent and confusing.

On this matter the UK government is a long way behind those of Australia, New Zealand and Ireland, which take a much more positive and relaxed attitude to LETS, seeing them as valuable community initiatives worthy of support, and making that position abundantly clear. The UK government, by way of contrast, can offer only 'benign neglect'.

What is needed is some positive action to clear the LETS idea of any suggestion that it is part of the black economy, or that people's income could be affected if they join a system. One obvious way forward is being proposed by the Local Authorities and LETS Information Exchange, which has suggested the government could amend the regulations relating to the Social Security Contributions and Benefits Act, and exempt the trading activities of LETS members from its definitions of work. LETS payments would then be excluded from being treated as either income or earnings derived from employment.

Under a proposed new definition of LETS, a system would be approved if the government was satisfied on three counts: that it was a local community-based system, that its primary concern was to help people maintain their labour skills and keep in touch with the job market, and that it was not a system run for profit. The advantage of such a change to regulations is that, in contrast to introducing new legislation, it could be effected in a relatively short time, perhaps as little as six months.

Another obvious need is for the collective wisdom that has been gained in the last few years to be made more accessible to members of existing and potential groups, to save them from reinventing the wheel. In this matter the Lets-Link umbrella bodies in England and Scotland have been valuable sources of advice and information, but are necessarily limited in what they can do, given their minimal human and financial resources. But while many LETS coordinators and core group members have been not only dedicated but extremely effective in carrying out their unpaid tasks, some systems have suffered from a lack of experience in key areas. While many people would not want to lose the informal, friendly ethos that characterizes so much LETS activity, a little training in certain key skills could go a long way to improving their effectiveness. Local authorities are just beginning to get interested in LETS training, and should by now have a pool of experienced tutors to draw on for any courses they might set up.

Like credit unions and community businesses, housing and food cooperatives, and other self-help schemes, LETS are increasingly being looked at for their potential for community development and for regenerating local economies. Several councils are now offering groups support as part of their anti-poverty or community development strategies. Others are doing so under the banner of Local Agenda 21, which invites communities to produce their visions for a more sustainable lifestyle by looking at such questions as ethical shopping, food and agriculture, economy and work, and others that overlap both practically and philosophically with LETS.

The involvement of local authorities in LETS is set to increase, possibly dramatically in some impoverished areas. But there is a widespread feeling that this will only be effective in the long term if it involves discreet support, rather than a heavy-handed 'top-down' imposition of the idea on a community. A LETS is essentially a personal system which allows individuals to determine more of their own lives, and anything that tends to diminish that element should be resisted.

Some people believe that LETS can only function in the mainstream economy if they attract many more members, and begin to draw in a significant number of businesses. LETS coordinating organizations trying to pilot schemes to involve small businesses can at present only scratch the surface, mainly through lack of funds. If businesses are to be persuaded of the value to them of a

LETS, their interest needs to be carefully nurtured. So this kind of sustained development work needs to be properly supported.

Will new technology provide a boost for LETS? Already use is being made of the Internet to access and exchange information. Yet one of the main aims and value of a LETS is that it brings individuals into personal contact with each other in a world that is increasingly impersonal and alienating. If technology is to be used at all, it should be kept under control, and never become the dominating element.

It's often said that a LETS can have a positive effect on a local economy. Yet so far there's little hard evidence to show that this has happened. Now that LETS have a track record, the moment seems ripe for a pilot scheme to be set up to identify that effect. Such a scheme was recently launched by the Department of Commerce and Trade in Australia. The aim was to increase the economic turnover of a depressed small town in Western Australia by 10 per cent in a year, using LETS trading. A similar initiative in the UK or Ireland, perhaps in contrasting rural and urban areas, could provide evidence of the real economic value of LETS, as well as of their cost as a means of effecting community regeneration.

Will LETS survive into the next century, or will they peter out as many other community-based initiatives have done? Certainly they have already brought significant benefits to thousands of people in the UK and Ireland. Nevertheless they have still touched only a tiny proportion of the population, and have yet to make a real impact on all but a few of the poorest and most disadvantaged members of our society.

Yet the essence of LETS fits snugly with the idea of sustainability, a concept which is slowly but increasingly being recognized as vital to the future of the planet. It also encourages people to respond to the well-worn slogan 'act locally, think globally', a practice which is likely to be as relevant to the survival of communities in the twenty-first century as it has been in the latter part of the twentieth.

REFERENCES

1 Ward, C (1995) Learning about LETS, *Raven*, no 31
2 Croall, J (1997) *LETS Act Locally: The Growth of Local Exchange Trading Systems*, Gulbenkian Foundation

FURTHER READING

Cole, M (1953) *Robert Owen of New Lanark*, Batchworth Press

Dauncey, G (1996) *After the Crash: The Emergence of the Rainbow Economy*, 2nd edn, Green Print

Dobson, R (1994) *Bringing the Economy Home from the Market*, Black Rose Books, Canada

Douthwaite, R (1996) *Short Circuit: Strengthening Local Economies in an Unstable World*, Green Books/Lilliput Press

Lang, P (1994) *LETS Work: Rebuilding the Local Economy*, Grover Books

PART VI

Fashioning a New Politics

10 THE PATH NOT (YET) TAKEN: THE POLITICS OF SUSTAINABILITY

Ken Worpole

A DIFFERENT KIND OF POLITICS

I think about a different kind of politics nearly every time I take a train journey out of the city. For shortly after the train has left the station and speeds up through the suburbs, one suddenly looks out on networks of allotments, caravan sites or tin-shed communities, where life appears, from a distance at least, independent and self-reliant: sometimes through necessity, sometimes by choice. The virtues of sturdy independence are politically in vogue again, and are often evoked as something peculiarly English. Of course they are not. Any train journey leaving from any city in the world will quickly bring you to landscapes where self-sufficiency and making do are still in evidence. The virtues and allegedly hidden cultures of small-scale self-sufficiency are rarely evoked in mainstream political cultures, but it may be that their time has finally come.

The historian Richard Cobb was one of the keenest witnesses to what can be understood and learned from these marginal territories, urging historians and others to,

> '. . . seek out the courtyards and workshops, the alleyways and closed passages, the semi-private, semi-secret cités or villas with iron gates to close them in at night, (and) search on foot, walking along abandoned railway lines, or little used canals, behind breakers' yards and small chaotic workshops, and industrial waste, the borderlands of cities, the gasworks, the cemeteries, the marshalling yards, and bus depots, and bus cemeteries, two-decker trams converted into houses and covered in greenery.

> *An apparently abandoned cottage may be just visible between*
> *thick tentacular creeper, still indicating life ... and the*
> *evidence of love and care in a tiny garden decorated with*
> *scallop-shells arranged in rings stuck in earth filling old petrol*
> *cans nestling against the high wire netting – la maison du*
> *sauvage, a small temple of individualism, an artisanal folly,*
> *by a Sunday architect.'* [1]

These vernacular landscapes, and the informal politics and social relations they represent, defy easy schematization. For many of us brought up in post-war Britain, politics has largely taken the form of either/or. Binary choices – in politics particularly – leave many of the most important, long-term issues unaddressed or unresolved, as all of the contributors to this book spell out. It is not so much the path not taken, to evoke Robert Frost's famous poem, as whether we should have gone into this particular wood at all.

Throughout the world where forms of representative democracy operate, the historic counter-oppositions – left and right, state and market, public and private, conservationist or developmental – are proving inadequate to cope with the complexity of the problems facing communities (including nation-states) and the choices which press upon them. The temptation to argue for a 'Third Way', straight down the middle, a classical ploy of populist politics, is even less convincing, as it employs a spatial metaphor to try to freeze what is always a dynamic and fluid set of social relations and understandings. Wittgenstein, another Sunday architect and backstreet wanderer, noted how the shape of the world, its assumed directionality and 'hidden purpose', was no longer amenable to a fixed interpretation, a point of view now widely accepted. In one of his notebooks he observed that:

> *'In the actual use of expressions we make detours, we go by*
> *side roads. We see the straight highway before us, but of course*
> *we cannot use it, because it is permanently closed.'* [2]

The straight highway is permanently closed – that is the principal argument of this book. Politics is no longer a clash of titans, a life and death struggle between rival ideologies or economic systems, but a matter of understanding the sheer complexity of the economic and social ecologies of the societies in which we live. In such ecologies, many quick-fix solutions may well produce 'revenge' effects, making the original problem even worse; given that many of the natural resources we are now consuming are irreplaceable, and the environmental effects irreversible, such a way of proceeding can no longer be taken for granted. Reflexivity, feedback, self-regulating and self-correcting loops of information and process, provisionality and cautionary optimism, now seem the hallmarks of successful political activity and change. Small is beautiful, but cautionary self-correction is best.

The fact that ecological metaphors are now being used to describe economic and social processes and systems is a clear sign of the recognition of the complexity, variability, and volatility of modern societies – and their vulnerability to unexpected systems failures and occasional human and environmental catastrophes. One small example helps us understand these wider systemic loops. In the UK, fears about child safety have led to an increasing number of parents driving their children to and from school each day. The presence of so many cars on the road at such peak times creates both the greater risk of traffic accidents involving injury to children, but also adds to the CO_2 pollution and the emission of fine particulates (PM10s), now associated with the growing increase of childhood asthma. Thus the means compromise the ends. The result is that 'safe-routes-to-school' programmes encouraging children to walk to school are now being set up around the country, and so walking becomes a radical – even innovative! – solution to a complex problem. *'The simple things, so difficult to achieve'*, Brecht once despaired.

This is a small example of such issues, but it sets the scene. We are surrounded by the problems caused by the wealth of choices available to us in a consumer economy, ranging from how we reconcile the desire to live in a semi-rural setting, with good schools and pleasant neighbours in close proximity, with the wishes of millions of others to do exactly the same; or the belief that we can somehow have a plentiful supply of cheap food and fashionable clothing while closing our eyes to the conditions of the animals bred in battery farms, or the wages and conditions of young children who work in sportswear factories in the developing world.

The connections between how we live, and the networks and systems of economic activity, human and resource exploitation which support that style of living, are now, often deliberately, occluded. Yet every so often crises erupt, such as the BSE scandal, or a whole river system is found to have become polluted by the run-off from a farm or factory and all the fish and wildlife destroyed, or rioting on a number of peripheral housing estates around the country 'suddenly' reveals the existence of cultures of despair and self-destruction in the midst of seeming plenitude. Such incidents remind us how dangerously close to the edge of social and environmental instability, or even disaster, we may be.

The gap between how we wish to live, and how this can be reconciled with longer-term issues of environmental sustainability and social cohesion, is enormous. The influential Marxist literary critic, George Lukacs, once said that we would one day regard the relationship between the individual and society as no more difficult to understand than the relationship between mind and body. This day has not yet arrived. If anything, the ability to assert such a relationship seems to grow even more difficult, particularly as some of the intermediary institutions – the extended family, the work-place and the neighbourhood – weaken or atrophy under the onslaught of economic individualism.

The sociologist, Anthony Giddens, has talked of the need '*to repair damaged solidarities*', as one of the principal tasks of politics today, while his French counterpart, Pierre Bourdieu, has written eloquently of the '*opportunity for the sociologist . . . to mend the crockery broken by economists*'.[3] Repairing and mending, refurbishing and renewing – these are the political imperatives not of some single-minded, thrusting, whatever-you-do-don't-look-back programme of increasing production and consumption, but of a different way of doing things, and another way of seeing. So while traditional right and left political systems are in deep disarray – with the failure of both *dirigiste* state planning on the one hand, and a growing disillusionment with the corrosive social and environmental effects of unregulated market forces on the other – there is a renewed interest in community-based, mutual-aid solutions.

Yet, as has already been argued, such broad movements remain largely invisible to conventional political analysis. A recent study by the American political scientist, Terry Nichols Clark, on the 'New Political Culture', while descriptively valuable, offers little sense of the overwhelming environmental imperative for seeking to shape public opinion and create new agencies for change.[4] Clark's schematization of certain kinds of global political trends towards greater citizen democracy; more issue-based politics; liberalism in social matters but economic individualism in fiscal matters; less universalist, more pluralistic, urban lifestyle politics – trends he perceives in the programmes of political parties and leaders in many parts of the world – *'remains a description of a political culture that paradoxically lacks a political culture to understand it'*.

There is nothing reflexive in such forms of political analysis; nor is there any sense of the necessary humility we need now to adopt in the face of the problems which lie ahead. Without a convincing story to tell ourselves about what kind of society we wish to live in, or in which direction we seek to go, we are likely to remain at the mercy of whichever economic and corporate winds might blow.

The contributors to this book all share the feeling that the winds of global capitalism blow too strongly, and continue to unleash on the world economic processes, supported by vast advertizing and marketing campaigns, which suggest that human well-being and high levels of personal consumption of goods and services are the same thing. According to the politicians, higher incomes and more consumer goods were supposed to produce happy families and cheerful neighbourhoods. Instead, the divisive effects of growing inequality in jobs, housing and disposable income, even when there has been an overall rise in gross domestic product (GDP), have tended to produce higher crime rates, dissatisfied and unstable family relationships, unsafe streets and neighbourhoods, and wide-spread pessimism about the future. Some recent international research has also supported this view that inequality in itself produces unhealthier societies, irrespective of actual levels of material well-being.[5]

Quality of Life: What Is It and Can It Be Measured?

It is for this reason that politicians and others (particularly environ-mentalists) no longer talk publicly about raising 'the standard of living', but instead talk about the need to secure a reasonable 'quality of life' (or what Bourdieu has called 'an economics of well-being'). The former assumes that the goal of politics is to carry on increasing individual quantitative wealth for ever, and the latter asks what is wealth for, and how is it related to what individuals and collectives perceive to be secure, stable and rewarding ways of living?[6] The two things are quite different, and it is this difference that is now the subject of changing government policies which seek to recreate some of the better characteristics of traditional, mutual aid and/or self-help 'organic' communities. Some of this is done in the name of communitarianism, some in the name of traditional values.

Creating 'community' is not easy, and here another recent example may help. In modern town planning, and in government policy, there is much talk of creating social mix in new housing developments – as if social mix were just another design factor to be bolted on. It is felt that successful social mix is a public good in its own right and could act as a brake upon individual anti-social behaviour. Yet there is quite a lot of evidence to suggest that new housing development in Britain is becoming even more socially polarized, as private developers prefer to pay fines, or make compensation available as 'planning gain', in order to build exclusive developments in one part of town, while the council uses the newly acquired funds to build social housing in another. In modern Britain we simply do not know how to create social mix, if we are honest with ourselves: demonstrating how political rhetoric simply cannot be backed up by example within conventional ways of doing things.

The collective 'feelgood' factor is much more difficult to produce than individual states of well-being. At least 'standard of living' is relatively easy to measure, whereas 'quality of life' is notoriously difficult to describe or ascertain. There now seem to be two schools of thought about how one might measure quality of life: one aggregates all the statistical evidence, and the other asks people how they feel. Differences – sometimes striking – between these approaches have engendered a debate which continues to this day. In one survey the following 20 qualities were ranked in order of importance by those asked about what most affected them in their assessment of a good quality of life:

- Violent crime
- Non-violent crime
- Health provision
- Pollution levels
- Cost of living
- Shopping facilities
- Racial harmony
- Scenic-quality, access
- Cost of owner-occupied housing
- Education provision
- Employment prospects

- Wage levels
- Unemployment levels
- Climate
- Sports facilities
- Travel-to-work time
- Leisure facilities
- Quality council housing
- Access council housing
- Cost of private-rented housing[7]

A sense of safety and security, particularly among women and on behalf of children, remains one of the key issues for social and urban policy today, and in many ways is regarded as a touchstone of successful communities. Yet it is precisely a quality that money cannot buy. It is one of the great intangibles wrapped up in the elusive concept of community, which so many evoke, but few can demonstrate to exist.

The startling fact which emerges from comparisons between 'objective' and 'subjective' surveys is that around certain key issues *there is hardly any correlation between a broad-based (and perception-influenced) ranking of quality of life and 'objective' local prosperity.* Given an agreed basic standard of living and set of expectations about the right to housing, education, work, and the other staples of life, all the differences between getting by and a sense of well-being are to be found in the intangibles.

Work is now being undertaken to develop ways of measuring some of these intangibles, through attention to such unexpected 'performance indicators' of well-being as well as membership of voluntary organizations, time spent with other people as opposed to time spent alone or watching television, attendance at live sports and cultural events and so on. The New Economics Foundation meanwhile has developed an 'Index of Sustainable Economic Welfare' to take account of the hidden environmental costs of current forms of production and consumption, and the Office for National Statistics has recently produced what it calls The Environmental Accounts for the UK. All these moves towards a more balanced way of understanding human welfare and well-being are to be welcomed, though one sometimes wonders why it has never been obvious before.

Yet the fact that many of the problems highlighted by new forms of accounting cannot be 'solved' by additional spending doesn't make things any easier for politicians anxious to save money. These perceptual worries are less amenable to traditional remedies, whereby the provision of a service or a set of public goods – houses, buses, hospitals, schools, roads, sewers – was simply a matter of political will and an ability to raise taxes. For we are now dealing with issues of social poverty rather than physical poverty, with the fear of neighbours rather than the fear of a punitive and authoritarian welfare state. In some places community development programmes are one response to these issues of social fragmentation, but adding another layer of professionals won't solve all the problems. No wonder that many politicians are now perplexed, having dedicated their lives to the provision of better public services and goods, only to find that the expected rewards of well-ordered and contented communities remain as elusive as ever, and that there is little left in their political armoury with which to address these new concerns. The 'repair of damaged solidarities', as cited above, is now a major political task, one requiring quite different forms and processes (and even rules) of engagement than before.

Where Do New Ideas Come From? The Importance of the Margins

But where are the new political and social ideas to come from? If societies and cultures are self-reproducing, how is it ever logically possible for any discrepant or innovative ideas to emerge, let alone get put into practice? Happily even the most self-regulating and internally policed cultures cannot but produce areas of marginality and dissonance. Human nature no more runs along tram lines than do the forms of social reproduction. And if there are centres of power, by definition there have to be margins too – places and spaces where the writ of the centralized power no longer rules or only rules weakly and sporadically. In this collection, marginality is celebrated. For many of the contributors to this book, marginality is held to be both a place and a kind of political temperament, where the novel, the experimental, the counter-intuitive can be explored. We are back to those allotments and Sunday architects again.

In 1986 the geographer Dennis Hardy organized a seminar at Middlesex Polytechnic on the theme of 'Marginality'. In many ways the seminar and the small publication which emerged from it exemplified marginality too – a quiet, thoughtful exchange of ideas with a small occasional paper issued subsequently in an edition of perhaps no more than 200 copies. Yet the papers were quite rich and profound, and their influence can still be seen to be spreading. In his introduction Hardy wrote convincingly about the importance of marginality:

> *'It is a truism to say that marginality is simply about those things which are not at the centre. It applies to what appears to be an increasing volume of activities which are not initiated by mainstream institutions, but which characteristically skirt around them. Marginal activities stem from the 'bottom up' rather than 'top down'. Such activities are not necessarily illegal (in most cases manifestly not), but will sometimes stretch legal interpretation to its limit, or will require new legislation to ratify what is already done.*
>
> *In the geographer's language, it is about life at the periphery rather than at the core. But marginality cannot be dismissed as being simply peripheral or, as some would have it, eccentric. Explanations of behaviour that is unconventional cannot be dismissed as mere whim. In fact, the reverse is true. The reasons for marginality are not to be found on the margins of society (where the activity itself occurs), but in the very core, for marginality can be seen as a reaction to weaknesses inherent in mainstream institutions. It is a positive response by people for whom the conventional workings of society have failed to deliver.'* [8]

The very phrase, life at the periphery, evokes for me powerful images and emotions, notably of those train journeys recounted at the beginning of this chapter. On a recent visit to Denmark I visited a number of 'kolonihaven' (garden colonies) in and around Copenhagen. One was a place where people now lived throughout the year, regardless of the law which regards colony life as a summer activity, and that particular journey to the margins was classically true to type. From the centre of the city we were directed to take the No 40 bus route out to Nokken – *'it's at the end of the line, you can't go any further'* said the people who had given us directions. At the last stop the few people left on the bus alighted and set off in various directions. A hundred yards or so ahead, in the direction we were going, the road literally came to an end, and then we walked across a couple of fields, finally arriving at a small community by the river, made up of wooden summer houses, workshops, allotments, connected to each other by gravel paths.

The success of Nokken – and the continuing development of 'The Free State of Christiana', a vast squatted army barracks and wooded hinterland in the centre of Copenhagen – has led the city government to re-consider its attitudes towards self-sufficient, self-build communities, and to ask whether the development of year-round 'kolonihaven' in and around the city might be a reasonable idea, as the lifestyles they encourage seem to be so environmentally benign. We also visited the adventure playground at Emdrup, established in 1946 to serve a housing estate to the north of the city, the first adventure playground ever. This was another marginal site, a piece of unused land left at the end of the development, and using marginal materials (old bits of timber, principally, which gave the original Danish name, 'junk playgrounds', translated more acceptably into adventure playgrounds for the English public).The Emdrup example inspired similar projects around the world, and is still thriving today.

Such marginal spaces and marginal experiments in living and working are richly inventive. Nearly all of the contributors to this book have worked on the margins – in free schools, community bookshops, organic farms, in small education and environmental projects in Britain and in the developing world – yet the lessons they have learned and the stories they have told now contain a powerful message for the centre. This is what begins to happen when you do things differently: it *is* possible to both conserve and develop, to learn and to play, to move beyond dependency, to do more for less, to value domestic work as much as work in the market-place, to be at home in both the country and the town. In short, there are ways of living which can begin to address the economic, social and environmental problems which increasingly face us, and which offer hope for the future if we patiently learn from them and modify policy and process accordingly.

Similarly we need to observe that all cultures create laboratories or places of experiment of various kinds. In art, this is the role played by the avant-garde, in science it is often the research institutes of the universities and large commercial companies – but in social relations (the most difficult area of all) it is among marginal communities and lifestyles, on the fringes of society, where the new experiments in living are explored. Many of these may be occurring in other countries, and at present many of the lessons on social policy seem to be coming from Denmark and the Netherlands. Why is it that small countries seem to be so much more innovative? In the 1980s and early 1990s all the new ideas about economic and social policy seemed to be coming from North America, and those of us directly involved in policy matters were urged to look across the Atlantic for the big picture. In reality, we may learn more from the many successful environmental and social initiatives emerging from Scandinavia and other European countries.

Colin Ward was one of the contributors to the 1986 Middlesex seminar, and to some extent the seminar was a gloss on a number of issues raised by his writings over the years. On the occasion of the Middlesex seminar, he chose to focus on the economic marginality of childcare, which

> *'if we had to pay people and institutions to care for all our children, like the rich do, then the whole gross domestic product of the United Kingdom would not be enough to meet the cost.'*[9]

Re-evaluating the importance of domestic work within the economy, and giving full recognition and esteem to the enormous amount of voluntary work that people do outside the home as well, in the form of community activity, care for the sick and the elderly, running clubs and societies, is another way of challenging the centre/periphery model in conventional economic thought.[10] Without the social glue of voluntarism and mutual aid, society would quickly unravel and not even the strictest disciple of economic liberalism could save it.

If new ideas tend to emerge from the margins and interstices of mainstream institutional life, there remains the problem of how they are disseminated. It is still surprising how little exposure to other kinds of ways of doing things and other kinds of institutions most people have in Britain, irrespective of class or geography. When I worked in a Hackney community centre in the early 1970s we created close links with a similar project in Liverpool, and began a series of exchanges and visits. Most Hackney people had never been to Liverpool before and most Liverpool people had never been to Hackney. Differences in attitudes, housing traditions, religion, politics, pub life, domestic rituals, and so on, many found quite startling and challenging. We mostly still gain a sense of 'things being different' from holidays abroad, but the differences and learning opportunities at home are often even more striking. In my own work on public library provision, I have been astonished how few people have ever used any other library than that nearest to them, and where provision is bad, simply do not realize what a good library service could be like. The same is true of the differences between the best and worst in housing management, in play provision, and so on. How can we know if there is a better way of doing things if our life-worlds are so entrenched and taken for granted?

Yet this is not an argument for standardization, or the central-ization of performance measures and auditing, which invariably end up as promoting as most beneficial those goods and services most amenable to measurement, as has been noted in the 'quality of life' argument. It is, rather, an argument for supporting local initiative, backed up by the dissemination of good ideas, good practice, and the opportunities for more people to share one another's experiences. Greater local autonomy is likely to lead to greater local distinctiveness, not less.

As David Goodway makes clear in Chapter 1, Colin Ward was exemplary in reporting back on the myriad small social experi-ments he saw or read about in the course of his work with *Anarchy* magazine and then *New Society*. It is difficult to over-estimate the importance of the role which *New Society* played in British culture, particularly in the 1960s and 1970s, under the initial editorship of Timothy Raison, and subsequently Paul Barker. *New Society* drew strongly on the best work in British sociology, particularly around issues of class, regionalism, changing demographic patterns and emergent lifestyles (including counter-cultures). It was also strongly ethnographic. It embodied a strong anti-collectivist mentality (Raison went on to become a Conservative MP) and was decidedly non-metropolitan.

Perhaps, as importantly, it was also committed to plain, and if not plain then energetic writing, and promoted writers and social critics such as Rayner Banham, John Berger, Angela Carter, David Donnison, Mary Douglas, Eva Figes, Ray Gosling, Colin MacInnes, Ray Pahl, Tony Parker, Sheila Rowbotham, Raphael Samuel, EP

Thompson, Raymond Williams and Michael Young, among others. If the tone of *The Spectator* was public-school table-talk from the smoky gloom of the pubs and clubs of metropolitan Fleet Street and Pall Mall, then the tone of *New Society* was decidedly more robust and muscular, owing much to Cobbett and Orwell, provincial in the best sense of the word, richly sociological and topographical, frequently outdoors.

In such propitious circumstances Ward's interests and pre-occupations came into their own. Whether he was writing about a free school in Liverpool, a self-build housing scheme in Lewisham, or reviewing a pamphlet about children's school strikes in London before the First World War, the attentiveness to the self-organized nature of the activities, and the small vignettes of enthusiasm and experimentation in unknown places, fitted in with the magazine's own espousal of the dissonant, awkward and anthropological within English culture rather than the metropolitan *qui vive*, or knowing self-consciousness.

Sometimes he simply wrote about his own intellectual influences and debts, and has indeed published a book of essays about the writers who have continued to influence him throughout his life:

> '*Personally, I have been endlessly lucky with influences. I left school at fifteen and consequently was not told what to read. Other writers chanced to lead me to them . . . My influences sought as wide an audience as possible. They did not all write particularly well, but they did address the reader as a serious person to be debated with, not as an ignoramus to be bullied or hectored. Still less did they pander to or flatter the prejudices or superstitions of their prospective readership. My major influences founded no parties. None of them started wars nor took part in governments. None of them inspired people to hate each other. All were utter failures in the entrepreneurial culture. But in my experience not a day passes when I fail to recall the influence of one or another of them, whether I am thinking about education, the organisation of work, about architecture and planning, the right use of land or of our inheritance of human resourcefulness and natural resources.*'[11]

THEMES AND CONCERNS

In this book, the contributors have all described areas of intellectual work and thought where Ward has opened up new paths. In the second half of this concluding essay I would like to outline a number of themes and concerns which have emerged in Ward's work and which seem to me to provide a set of issues which are likely to gain importance in any new politics that takes environmental and social sustainability seriously.

Childhood and Human Play

Ward's most influential and best known book is *The Child in the City* first published in 1978.[12] This book is always a delight to read again, so powerful is the case it makes for the importance of the early childhood need to explore and to feel at home in his or her locality and environment. Early in the book Ward quotes a childhood reminiscence by an American museum director, Albert Parr, recalling his early years in a Norwegian seaport at the turn of the century, when as a four-year-old he was often sent to the docks to buy fish, and in the course of his errand would visit the railway station, watch the trains, call in at the park to watch the band play, wander by the fire station to feed the horses, before returning home with his goods. The story is a staple of many of Ward's talks to teachers and educationalists, as I recall from hearing him for the first time in 1973 when I was teaching in Hackney and attended a talk of his as part of my in-service training, and 20 years later at a seminar at the Architectural Association.

Cynics can find all kinds of reasons why such an experience is *sui generis*, and untranslatable into any other time or culture. Yet while writing this chapter I was also enjoying a newly published memoir by Firmin Rocker, *The East End Years: A Stepney Childhood*, in which the author similarly recalls having the freedom of the streets at the age of three (and Jamaica Street, Stepney, where the author's family lived was regarded as pretty fearsome territory at the time).[13] While the age at which children were allowed to explore the streets may now shock us, the issue today is no longer at what age, but if at all.

There is now some hard thinking and self-questioning going on as to what as a society we have done to the experience of childhood. The pervasive fear of crime (which may not be supported by statistical evidence, although crime and crime statistics often exist in a kind of self-reinforcing loop), allied to traffic danger, has led to many children being prevented from going out and about in their neighbourhoods, whether by bike, bus or on foot, with a resultant loss of street skills, and an increasingly diminished sense of discovery and pleasure.[14] Child experts now talk of 'battery' children and 'free-range' children – the latter being those who are allowed out to play and apparently show signs of being healthier, more autonomous and more content.[15]

Putting childhood centre-stage, may perhaps be anarchism's (and Ward's) single most important contribution to social policy and political thought. The concern with the childhood experience is always unswervingly there in Ward's writings and concerns. He links it to the importance of play, which in the writings of the Dutch historian Johanes Huizinga, in the work of the educational psychologist Jean Piaget, in the educational writings and experiments of Homer Lane, AS Neill, and Caldwell Cook, as well as in the earlier writings of Jean-Jacques Rousseau and Wordsworth, is seen as essential to the creation of the elementary forms of sociability, a sense of justice and civic responsibility.[16] Ward's ludic imagination also helps explain his love of building things, for in like vein, Witold Rybczynski in his recent book about architecture, *The Most Beautiful House in the World*, has a marvellous historical chapter on games, toys and building games, as the formative stages of the architectural and creative disposition.[17]

The great secular trinity of love, play and freedom, which those of us who trained to be teachers in the 'permissive' 1960s took on as a set of over-riding principles for individual and social well-being, looks even more attractive and robust than ever. Damaged childhoods produce damaged, dependent and destructive adult cultures, and any sustainable politics has to take the experience of childhood centrally and seriously. Eileen Adams' chapter on the Art and the Built Environment Project, which Ward helped initiate in the 1970s, puts active exploration and 'streetwork' at the centre of environmental education. If anything, this kind of physical exploration is more urgently needed now than ever, as so often at home children are kept locked up with consumer goods as compensation for not being allowed to have the freedom of the streets around them.

The Return of 'the Local'

The freedom of the child to roam and play, to learn through discovery and exploration of the physical environment, puts a high value on the importance of the local and its symbolic meaning as human habitat. In the heady days of post-modern global social theory, the central argument of which was that in the world of instant electronic communication, traditional concepts of time and space are abolished, some urbanists seemed willing to dispense with the concept of the local altogether. Our ability to travel with ease, to communicate across the world, to work at considerable distances from where we live, and to spend much of our leisure watching television programmes beamed from satellites circling overhead, appears to render local space meaningless.

But this very process of atomization and deracination has produced environmental and social effects that are now being countered by a 'return to the local' as a place where values are created in their most dynamic and important ways – through an acknowledgement of the importance of safe play; through neighbourly cooperation; through the LETS schemes described by Jonathan Croall in Chapter 9; through the collective forms of provision of public goods – parks, libraries, swimming pools, institutional architecture, public streets and squares – which provide the social glue and infrastructure central to any possibility of sustainability, and hence the centrality to modern politics of Local Agenda 21. As Wordsworth wrote in The Prelude:

> 'Not in Utopia – subterranean fields –
> Or some secreted island, Heaven knows where!
> But in the very world, which is the world
> Of us all – the place where, in the end,
> We find our happiness, or not at all!'

The rise of environmental organizations, which emphasize the importance of the local, such as Common Ground, Groundwork, broad-based community organizing movements associated with the Foundation for Civil Society, the Development Trusts Association, as well as the proliferation of Local Agenda 21 initiatives, together with the importation of new concepts of neighbourhood-planning such as 'home zones' from The Netherlands, all attest to this renewed interest in the local as the testing ground for other ways of working and living.

To those who doubt whether there is any value in taking locality seriously in a world of global movement and migration, it is still worth remembering that over half of British adults live within five miles of where they were born, and even Britain's many newly established ethnic minority communities are highly localized, and often choose to remain so.[18] As the geographer Doreen Massey has asserted on many occasions, the local is ever-present and imbued with meaning in all cultures, even though some people simult-aneously – or separately – inhabit other spaces and time zones.

Out In The Open

The arcadian temperament which informs Ward's interests and studies reflects a clear preference for the greater democracy and sociability of life outdoors. The divide between indoor and outdoor mentalities and social pre-occupations is likely to become an inter-esting new area of political concern, as the politics of sustainability is seen to be on a collision course with the market-driven imperative to put more and more human activity indoors – with controlled access, controlled climate, and electronic personal and demo-graphic profiling an integral feature of entry and use. This is now increasingly the case with shopping, sport and leisure (indoor cricket, bowls, tennis, and the phenomenal growth of personal fitness centres), with the new generation of holiday villages (which make a feature of climate-controlled pool/café and sports areas with indoor vegetation), and the popularity of home-centred, computer-based work and leisure. Such lifestyles require enormous amounts of energy to keep them going. They are usually car-based, and need continuous lighting, heating, air-conditioning, security and electronic surveillance. Meanwhile the quality of maintenance and management of parks and public open spaces (including out-door markets) continues to decline in many British towns and cities.

The detailed interest in the history and role of allotments, which Colin Ward and his collaborator David Crouch turned into a standard work of social history, is very much about the interplay of self-sufficiency, self-management and the pleasures of the out-doors (principally for men) in urban cultures.[19] To its credit the new Labour government has already begun to conduct an enquiry into the future of allotments, although one of the major issues at present is not about increasing provision, but about whether allotment sites protected by local by-laws might be made available, if under-used, for building more houses. The local production of food is becoming an important political issue, and one covered persuasively in Chapter 8 by Tim Lang.

Ward's interest in the plotland developments in the early part of this century, in which homeless or ill-housed individuals and families built their own homesteads and established small-holdings on cheap rural land, is another aspect of this interest in self-sufficiency, and the outdoor life. It is also there in his work as Education Officer at the TCPA and the advocacy of street-based exploration and discovery, the continuing interest in adventure playgrounds and open space planning. Reasserting the value of the pleasures of the outdoors, of the social mix of the street, the city centre, the park, and of course the seaside beach, is another emerging development of our times which is likely to play out in all kinds of interesting ways. This contrasts with the more formal social relations of institutional life (with the attendant cultural and class 'threshold factors' which prevent so many people from entering art galleries, museums, theatres and concert halls – but significantly not public libraries). As my father used to say, *'An hour outdoors is worth a day inside.'*

Valuing the Vernacular

Ward's interests and passions have contrived to keep him uniquely separate from the usual political formations of binary Britain. He is a lover of the natural world and the countryside who also delights in the achievements of the new towns, a social historian who thinks we are too constrained by the past, a utopian thinker whose image of the golden age to come might well be a piece of derelict land in the city where children make dens and tree houses from old oil drums and railway sleepers, and have access to a stand-pipe. His anarchist politics has meant that he has simply never fitted into the usual niches, let alone command positions of British intellectual and political life. His starting point on every issue has been the needs and concerns of people, particularly those with very little material wealth or status, yet whose ingenuity and common decency often underpin the foundations of 'British values'.

It is therefore entirely appropriate that his essay (Chapter 5) tackles headlong one of the single most contentious issues in contemporary politics, which is the alleged divide, or long-standing incompatibility, between town and country interests and concerns. Ward will have none of it. He has never been seduced by the aesthetic of the picturesque, or rural arcadia, in which there are few, if any, people to be seen, and the only buildings are melancholy classical ruins and broken temples. Neither is he persuaded by the charm of bucolic coaching inns and red-faced men in pink hunting jackets. In his books on plotlands, on holiday camps, on the child in the country, he endorses Raymond Williams' delight in a 'working landscape', where people find their own ways of settling into different kinds of landscapes and cultivating, building and earning an appropriate livelihood. Making and mending is what most people do best and what somehow always seems to cause the least long-term damage. Not only does he find pleasure in the vernacular landscapes of a working countryside, he also fully understands why town and city dwellers should also want to enjoy such landscapes from time to time, and in their own distinctive ways. In *Arcadia For All*, written with Dennis Hardy, he quotes at length the then well-known philosopher CEM Joad, thought to be very progressive at the time, complaining in the 1930s about:

> ' . . . the hordes of hikers cackling insanely in the woods, or singing raucous songs as they walk arm in arm at midnight down the quiet village street. There are people, wherever there is water, upon sea-shores or upon river banks, lying in every attitude of undressed and inelegant squalor, grilling them-selves, for all the world as if they were steaks, in the sun. There are tents in meadows and girls in pyjamas dancing beside them to the strains of the gramophone, while stinking disorderly dumps of tins, bags, and cartons bear witness to the tide of invasion for weeks after it has ebbed; there are fat girls in shorts, youths in gaudy ties and plus-fours, and a roadhouse round every corner and a cafe on top of every hill for their accommodation.'[20]

This contempt for young city people is an abiding refrain of the conservative rural idiom, though it is often shared by the Left's deep puritanism and fear of popular pleasure. Such attitudes are still deeply embedded today, as it becomes clear that while Britain's cities are multi-cultural and cosmopolitan, its counties and rural hinterlands are most certainly not. Research has shown that many ethnic minorities in Britain still feel uncomfortable in rural Britain, and this will not be overcome unless, like Ward, we continue to argue for the pleasures of the vernacular landscape, and the ability of the countryside to adapt to a multiplicity of new uses, especially around those of livelihood, self-sufficiency, and forms of popular leisure such as walking, cycling, camping, which in the long term may be more environmentally friendly than life indoors.[21]

Making and Mending

Another great Ward theme is self-sufficiency, or the culture of making and mending. This is clearly evident in his work on the plotlanders and the self-build housing movement, as well as his understanding of the importance to children of self-activity and constructional free play. But it also draws on a long tradition of what his long-standing colleague and friend, the sociologist Ray Pahl, has called the culture of 'self-provisioning'. Pahl's own research has shown in microcosm the enormous amount of self-provision which goes on in any community, through allotment-holding, fishing and poaching in rural or coastal communities, and the general neighbourly exchange of goods and services, which are now becoming more formalized through the LETS schemes, which are a recent and remarkable phenomenon of the self-help tradition (see Chapter 9).

Pahl is also sympathetic to children being allowed to work in various ways at an early age, if they so wish, since some of them seem to enjoy doing so for the air of independence it brings, but more importantly for the social and self-determining skills which it engenders. Having taught in a boys' school in Hackney for a number of years, it was frequently obvious to me that what many of the most troublesome teenagers badly needed was the opportunity to be in adult company, and were desperate for the 'freedom' which they saw embodied in the formal and informal economy. It was not uncommon to witness a truculent and moody 14-year-old in a mutilated school uniform miraculously transformed into an affable and witty human being on a Saturday, while working at the market stall or changing tyres at the garage: for all the world like the adults they actually believed they were. The child's deep wish for parity of esteem and autonomy, whether through play or work, is something which Ward and Pahl have argued for consistently; it is also strongly echoed by Fiona Carnie in Chapter 2.

The culture of looking after yourself, avoiding dependency and patronage, is often still to be found in poorer communities, but it has been systematically eroded by welfarism over the years, and the social costs are everywhere in evidence in what is now called 'the dependency culture', deplored by those who were once so assiduous in its promotion. Indeed, Meekosha, quoted in the recent study, *Community and Sustainable Development*, points to current government funding programmes in which *'groups become trapped by the need to continue to demonstrate oppression or disadvantage or victim status for funding purposes.'*[22] This reminds me of the town hall I once visited where in one room the tourist department spent all its time promoting the pleasures of the city and its lively, friendly people, while next door in the economic development department, others spent all their time filling in government forms demonstrating how impoverished and oppressed the city and its inhabitants had now become.

Wherever he looks Pahl still sees evidence of the making-and-mending culture, and of forms of self-help, arguing that *'the traditional English individualism now finds expression more in self-provisioning – in DIY home and car maintenance – than in formal employment.'*[23] Today this tradition is stronger in ethnic minority communities where the local economy, and the intense circulation of services in tiny geographical areas, is still vibrant. Some of these habits have been imported from other countries and cultures where self-employment is a much stronger tradition. For example one-third of the Turkish and Greek labour markets is self-employed; in Norway and Austria it is one-twentieth. Estimates of the size of the informal economy vary from six per cent of the official economy in Switzerland, 12 per cent in the UK, 24 per cent in Italy to 100 per cent in Russia.[24] The difficulty many first- and second-generation immigrants have in entering the formal labour market accounts for the strength of the informal economy in such communities.

The renewed political interest in that area of life which spans the informal economy, the social economy, voluntary work, the free exchange of goods and services, domestic work and child care, is the final acknowledgement of official political culture that the themes which Ward and others have been promoting for so many years are now being taken seriously. Both George Monbiot and Nicola Baird in Chapters 6 and 7 respectively, based on their own direct experience of working in developing countries, emphasize how much we, in the so-called developed world, have to learn from places where barter, exchange and self-sufficiency are still vital forms within the larger economy, despite the many attempts by multi-national firms to impose market relations and economics upon them.

Commons and Customs

Ward's anarchism has been strongly antagonistic to most forms of state provision, and some writers, myself included, do not always share this particular antipathy. As Alison Ravetz remarks in Chapter 4 on housing policy, public housing in Britain has continued to meet large-scale housing need, often at levels of quality not equalled by the market. I continue to believe that there are many vital services and institutions, usually in the form of public goods such as parks, libraries, street architecture, and even public order itself, which cannot be secured other than by some form of collective provision and civic management. Ward's most recent book, *Reflected in Water: A Crisis of Social Responsibility*,[25] moves some way towards acknowledging the more benign role that public, regulated, provision can play in adjudicating needs and interests over and above market or individualistic imperatives.

Ward, though, denies this interpretation. He claims to belong to the classical European anarchist tradition of Proudhon and Kropotkin, distinguishing between government and local administration. This view sees the modern centralized state as a despotic intrusion on the older provincial traditions of the commune. He wants to replace the state by a federation of communes on the Swiss pattern, and frequently declares that with the collapse of the Soviet Empire, Britain has become the most centralized state in Europe (a view with which the right-wing commentator, Simon Jenkins, would agree, and which he details in his recent book, *Accountable to None*[26]). Ward has argued since the 1960s for the take-over of local-authority housing in Britain by tenant cooperatives, and in 1974, anticipating the Thatcherite 'Right to Buy' policy, wrote a chapter in his book *Tenants Take Over*, called 'One by one, or all together?'[27] Similarly he claims that if control of water had remained local, this service could not have been sold to speculators in 1989.

But the issue at stake – how to find some kind of rapprochement between individual responsibility, collective self-management, and disinterested state provision – is likely to test political systems for some time to come, even though the moves at last seem to be going in the right direction: that is to say towards more mutual, more localized (where appropriate), and more participatory forms of decision-making and management.

The connection between political forms and the long term viability of what people are now calling 'sustainable communities' is largely tied up in the debate about 'common pool resources' and the need to secure the greater good (including the interests of future generations) over and above the sum of individual needs and interests in the here-and-now. A recent paper by the economist Tony Curzon Price, *How Can Natural Beauty Survive?*, based on looking at the success of different kinds of local political systems in preserving common interests, is highly pertinent here. The writer examines how French, Italian and Swiss alpine villages have managed to preserve their character and identity in the face of tourist pressures (and therefore pressures on local individuals to maximize their own financial interests). He concludes that:

> '*Swiss institutions of participative democracy, of radical local government autonomy, can be credited with avoiding the potential tragedy of the commons, and conversely, that the (poorly) representative system of local government in France* [and to a lesser extent in Italy – my addition] *has exacerbated the problem.*'[28]

Ward's book on water[29] owes some of its underlying political philosophy to Richard Titmuss's comparative international study of the blood transfusion service, *The Gift Relationship*,[30] which provided convincing evidence that a voluntary transfusion service was much cheaper, safer and more efficient than any service which either relied on payment to donors, or semi-compulsory donation by 'captive' or subaltern groups such as prisoners or military personnel. The disbenefits which have arisen in the change from seeing access to clean, safe water as a public right, to now seeing it as a commodity to be bought, and which can be more easily cut off in the case of non-payment, or squandered as long as you can pay for it, are now evident.

Yet it continues to be widely assumed that in most human endeavour the profit motive remains the driving force for innovation and large-scale accessibility of goods and services. Not so, at all, asserts Douglas Rushkoff, one of the most acerbic commentators on new technology:

> *'It is not the brute force of the market-place that has brought us any of the major technological and social leaps leading to what we now know as the Internet. These innovations have been driven by co-operation, not competition.*
>
> *The technologies behind e-mail, newsgroups, the Web browser and chat were not developed by companies, but by universities. They were not sold in stores, but distributed as shareware, for free. They were developed not by people looking to make money, but by students, teachers, and researchers hoping to advance the state of networked culture. These standards were not set by business monopoly or "first to market" incumbencies, but by committee . . . The fact remains that every single major development in online technology and communication came as shareware.'*[31]

What seems to be emerging in these debates about the values of collective provision, mutual aid, or self-help forms of provision, is that the freer the resources and the arrangements for using them are, the clearer and more publicly debated and acknowledged the rules of provision need to be.

Developing agreed rules of provision is one of the more interesting, if contentious, issues of current social policy. It is emerging in the attempt by local authorities to agree with housing tenants codes of conduct for good neighbourliness, and what is considered acceptable or unacceptable behaviour on estates (with sanctions attached!). Rules of provision are weakly there in various Citizens' Charters which publish a kind of contract with users, and funders, of public services as to what levels of service and efficiency can be expected in return for their taxes. Most LETS groups, as is clear from Chapter 9, have developed a simple set of rules as a framework for trading, which people can understand easily, and which are rarely broken. The newer wildlife trusts and ecology gardens have rules about appropriate and inappropriate activities in the interests of the particular local ecology – in contrast to municipal parks which remain intensely rule-bound (you can still find notice-boards pasted with minute by-law text dominating every entrance in some parks) yet whose rules are laid down without local consent and are largely unenforced.

There are rules, once moral and informal but now increasingly codified and subject to litigation, about intellectual copyright. In the wider spread of enlightenment and understanding, people felt free to incorporate other people's ideas, with acknowledgement where appropriate, and with elaboration and modification as necessary. The principles of scientific understanding included the need to diffuse knowledge as widely as possible, and all new innovators and discoverers acknowledged that they stood on the shoulders of the giants who went before them. Yet today there are forces in the world which seek to capture the fruits of knowledge, to patent them, and to increase their value not by diffusion but by suppression and privileged access. Against this, the contributors in this book assert that knowledge, like life, is a gift, and that this fragile earth will only survive if people learn to share and cooperate more with each other – despite all the difficulties attendant upon these processes – rather than seek to go their own way entirely and leave the rapacious forces of global free-market economics unchallenged and devoid of counter-arguments and other models of how things might be.

Colin Ward has been one of the greater sharers of knowledge, given freely, and the most non-litigious person one might ever wish to meet. This is truly the great strength of his anarchism and attitude to life: that sharing and giving freely, within the context of formal and informal networks of friends, colleagues and readers in general, is the most productive and sustainable kind of intellectual culture of all. He is known, admired and loved widely, because all of his work has been in its way a political gift to others, without hectoring, or rhetoric. His close attention to what might be learned from the study of peripheral spaces, to marginal economies, and alternative lifestyles, is likely to become increasingly influential. The lesson we might learn then is that individuals can, and do, make a difference, and so can the readers of this book.

NOTES AND REFERENCES

1 Cobb, R (1980) *Promenades*, Oxford University Press, p 3

2 Wittgenstein, trans Anscombe, GEM (1953) *Philosophical Investigations*, New York: cited in Geertz, C (1993) *Local Knowledge*, London: Fontana Press

3 The quotation by Anthony Giddens comes from Giddens, A (1994) *Beyond Left and Right: The future of radical politics*, Polity, p 12. The remarks by Pierre Bourdieu come from A Reasoned Utopia and Economic Fatalism in *New Left Review* no 227

4 Clark, TN (1998) 'Urban governance and the new political culture', a seminar given at Demos, London on 23 March 1998

5 Wilkinson, R (1996) *Unhealthy Societies: The Afflictions of Inequality*, Routledge

6 For a more detailed discussion of these differences see MacGillivray, A, Turning the Sustainability Corner: How to Indicate Right in Warburton, D (ed) (1998) *Community and Sustainable Development*, Earthscan. MacGillvray's work at the New Economics Foundation has been crucial in airing these debates about other ways of measuring economic well-being. See also Durning, AT (1994) *How Much is Enough?*, London: Earthscan; and, Gabriel, Y and Lang, T (1995) *Unmanageable Consumer*, Sage

7 Rogerson RJ, Findlay AM and Morris AS (1989) 'Indicators of Quality of Life: some methodological issues', *Environment & Planning*, vol 21. That 'fear of crime' is the main concern of many people when questioned about social attitudes is also endorsed by the 1994 British Crime Survey: Home Office (1996) *Anxieties about Crime* and Beck, A and Willis, A (1995) *Security: Managing the Risk to Safe Shopping*, Perpetuity Press

8 Hardy, D (1986) *On the Margins: Marginal Space and Marginal Economies*, Geography and Planning Papers no 17, Middlesex Polytechnic

9 Ibid

10 For further thoughts on this issue see Benn, M (1998) *Livelihood: work in the new urban economy*, Comedia/Demos and Coyle, D (1997) *The Weightless World*, Capstone Press (particularly ch 4, Nourishing the Grass Roots)

11 Ward, C (1991) *Influences: Voices of Creative Dissent*, Green Books, p 11

12 Ward, C (1978) *The Child in the City*, Architectural Press: published by Penguin Books (1979); reprinted by Bedford Square Press (1990)

13 Rocker, F (1998*) The East End Years: A Stepney Childhood*, London: Freedom Press

14 The most compelling research evidence for this portrait of sheltered and protected childhoods is contained in Hillman, M (1993) *Children, Transport and the Quality of Life*, London: Policy Studies Institute

15 See Hugill, B (1998) 'Minded Out of Their Minds', *The Observer*, 29 March

16 I have recently tried to follow up and elaborate upon this rich train of thought in Worpole, K (1998) *Nothing to Fear? Trust and Respect in Urban Communities*, Comedia/Demos

17 Rybczynski, W (1990) *The Most Beautiful House in the World*, USA: Penguin Books

18 This remarkable statistic is cited in Diane Warburton's introduction to Warburton, D (ed) (1998) *Community and Sustainable Development*, London: Earthscan

19 Crouch, D and Ward, C (1988) *The Allotment: Its Landscape and Culture*, Faber & Faber; new edition (1997) Nottingham: Five Leaves Books

20 Hardy, D and Ward, C (1984) *Arcadia for All: The Legacy of a Makeshift Landscape*, Mansell, p 40

21 See, for example, Young, L (1995) 'Environmental Images and Imaginary Landscapes', *Soundings* 1, Autumn, London

22 Warburton, D ed (1998) op cit, Note 18

23 Pahl, R 'Getting By, Survival Strategies or Liberating Lifestyles', in Hardy, D (ed) (1986) op cit, Note 8, p 9

24 Figures taken from an *Economist* survey, quoted in *The Guardian*, 3 January 1998

25 Ward, C (1997) *Reflected in Water: A Crisis of Social Responsibility*, London: Cassell

26 Jenkins, S (1995) *Accountable to None: The Tory Nationalization of Britain*, Hamish Hamilton

27 Ward, C (1974) *Tenants Take Over*, London: The Architectural Press

28 Price, TC, How Can Natural Beauty Survive?, essay in Barnett, A and Scruton, R (1998) *Town and Country*, London: Cape

29 Ward, C (1997) op cit, Note 24

30 Titmuss, R (1973) *The Gift Relationship: From Human Blood to Social Policy*, Harmondsworth: Penguin Books
31 Rushkoff, D (1998) Free lessons in innovation, *The Guardian*, 9 April

INDEX

Italics indicate articles and publications